TIME WITH GOD

PERSONAL Journal

WORD BIBLES

Dallas · London · Vancouver · Melbourne

TIME WITH GOD PERSONAL JOURNAL

Copyright © 1993 by Word Publishing, Inc. All rights reserved.

Scripture text taken from *The Holy Bible, New Century Version*. Copyright © 1987, 1988, 1991 by Word Publishing. All rights reserved. No part of this publication may be reproduced, stored in a retrieval system, or transmitted in any form or by any means – electronic, mechanical, photocopy, recording, or any other – except for brief quotations in printed reviews, without the prior written permission of the publisher.

All quotations shown on daily reading pages are listed with proper credit line in the Acknowledgments section at the end of the journal.

INTRODUCTION

Do you ever wish you could put your thoughts on paper? Have you had prayer concerns you would like to "keep track of"?

The *Time With God Personal Journal* has been created just for you. Each daily page contains a verse for the day, a thought for the day and lots of room for you to write your special insights, thoughts and prayer needs. The scripture verses are taken from the New Testament with references to the Old Testament included. As you fill in the pages and study the scriptures you will see by the end of your personal journal that you have read and studied the entire New Testament. It's a great way to combine daily Bible study with your own personal insights into God's Word.

Maybe you're having problems at work, pressures at home, family concerns, a special friend you have been praying for, or simply want to keep track of your daily devotional needs. Your *Time With God Personal Journal* follows the format of the popular *Time With God* one-year devotional, the New Testament for busy people. This daily devotional features the New Century Version, an accurate and easy-to-read Bible translation well-suited for daily readings.

Also included on each journal page are thoughts from well-known Christian authors such as Charles Swindoll, Billy Graham, Martin Luther and R. C. Sproul pertaining to that day's scripture reading. The personal journal will also be a welcome addition for your group Bible study or Sunday School classes.

We invite you now to begin studying a few minutes each day and keep track of your own thoughts and prayer concerns as you reflect on God's Word in your life.

Date _____

WEEK 1 / Monday

Verse of the Day

"You will name him Jesus, because he will save his people from their sins."

Matthew 1:21

Thought for the Day

God has given us the means to know the truth. Jesus is the way to the Father, because He is Our Redeemer.

Terry Fullan

Matthew 1:1-25
Isaiah 7:13-14

WEEK 1 / Tuesday

Date _____

Verse of the Day

They asked, "We saw his star in the east and have come to worship him."

Matthew 2:2

Thought for the Day

God is leading! This is my confidence and joy... my rest.

Richard Halverson

Matthew 2:1-23
Micah 5:2-5a

Date _____

Week 1 / Wednesday

Verse of the Day

"This is my Son, whom I love, and I am very pleased with him."

Matthew 3:17

Thought for the Day

God's promise, my submission.

Richard Halverson

Matthew 3:1-4:11
Pslam 34:11-14

WEEK 1 / Thursday

Date _____

Verse of the Day

Jesus said, "Come follow me, and I will make you fish for people."

Matthew 4:19

❦

Thought for the Day

To follow Christ is to abdicate the throne of our heart . . .

John Stott

Matthew 4:12-5:12

Genesis 12:1, 2, 4

Date _____

WEEK 1 / Friday

Verse of the Day

You should be a light for other people.

Matthew 5:16

Thought for the Day

If we are to be salt and light in our world, we need to go where the lost are.

Robert Tamasy

Matthew 5:13-37
Psalm 97:10-11

WEEK 1 / Weekend   Date _____

Verse of the Day

Forgive us for our sins, just as we have forgiven those who sinned against us.

Matthew 6:12

❦

Thought for the Day

Sin is a continuing problem, even for the believer.

J. Oswald Sanders

Matthew 5:38-6:15

Psalm 25:4-7

Date _____

WEEK 2 / Monday

Verse of the Day

So don't worry about tomorrow, because tomorrow will have its own worries.

Matthew 6:34

❦

Thought for the Day

Our problem is that we want to test God rather than trust him.

Al Bryant

Matthew 6:16-7:6

Nehemiah 9:1-3

Week 2 / Tuesday

Date _____

Verse of the Day

Ask, and God will give to you. Search, and you will find. Knock, and the door will open for you.

Matthew 7:7

❦

Thought for the Day

Let us put our hand in His, that He may lead us into the path of life.

F.B. Meyer

Matthew 7:7-8:4
Psalm 1:1-3

Date _____

WEEK 2 / Wednesday

Verse of the Day

Then Jesus got up and gave a command to the wind and the waves, and it became completely calm.

Matthew 8:26

❦

Thought for the Day

He is the omnipotent redeemer of His creation.

R. C. Sproul

Matthew 8:5-27

Psalm 104:1-4, 31-33

WEEK 2 / Thursday

Date _____

Verse of the Day

"I did not come to invite good people but to invite sinners."

Matthew 9:13b

❦

Thought for the Day

Redemption through the love of the Son of God is a theme without parallel in the world's religions.

J.I. Packer

Matthew 8:28-9:17

Psalm 103:8-13

Date _____

WEEK 2 / Friday

Verse of the Day

"There are many people to harvest but only a few workers to help harvest them."

Matthew 9:37

Thought for the Day

Jesus entered this world on a search-and-rescue mission for sinners.

John F. MacArthur, Jr.

Matthew 9:18-10:10
Ezekiel 34:15-16

Week 2 / Weekend

Date _____

Verse of the Day

"God even knows how many hairs are on your head. So don't be afraid."

Matthew 10:30-31

Thought for the Day

God is taking it all in. He has already appointed a prosecuting attorney, a jury, and a judge.

Charles Stanley

Matthew 10:11-40
Jeremiah 20:8c-9

Date _____

WEEK 3 / Monday

Verse of the Day

"Those who give one of these little ones a cup of cold water because they are my followers will truly get their reward."

Matthew 10:42

❦

Thought for the Day

God's kingdom is a synonym for God's rule.

Charles Swindoll

Matthew 10:41-11:24

Proverbs 1:22a, 24-26a, 28-31

WEEK 3 / Tuesday

Date _____

Verse of the Day

"Come to me, all of you who are tired and have heavy loads, and I will give you rest."

Matthew 11:28

❦

Thought for the Day

"Just give me a tear–a heart ready to mold. And I'll give you a mission, a message so bold."

Max Lucado

Matthew 11:25-12:21

Psalm 51:17

Date _____

WEEK 3 / Wednesday

Verse of the Day

"The mouth speaks the things that are in the heart."

Matthew 12:34b

Thought for the Day

What we talk about all the time is what we love.

Karen Burton Mains

Matthew 12:22-45

Proverbs 10:20-21

WEEK 3 / Thursday

Date _____

Verse of the Day

"But those who do not have understanding, even what they have will be taken away from them."

Matthew 13:12b

Thought for the Day

The fool despises wisdom and says in his heart there is no God. He will not hear.

John F. MacArthur, Jr.

Matthew 12:46-13:17

Zechariah 7:11-12

Date _____

WEEK 3 / Friday

Verse of the Day

"I will tell things that have been secret since the world was made."

Matthew 13:35b

Thought for the Day

God taught me more on my knees than I ever could have learned in all the seminaries or colleges in the world.

Woodrow Kroll of Andrew Frazer

Matthew 13:18-43

Deuteronomy 11:18-21

WEEK 3 / Weekend

Date _____

Verse of the Day

When he found a very valuable pearl, he went and sold everything he had and bought it.

Matthew 13:46

❦

Thought for the Day

The Kingdom of God. . . we must pray for it, and we must work for it.

Tony Campolo

Matthew 13:44-14:12

Psalm 145:10-13a

Date _____

WEEK 4 / Monday

Verse of the Day

And Peter left the boat and walked on the water to Jesus.

Matthew 14:29

Thought for the Day

When trusting God, there is nothing to fear.

Millie Stamm

Matthew 14:13-36

Psalm 116:5-9

Week 4 / Tuesday Date _____

Verse of the Day

What people say with their mouths comes from the way they think.

Matthew 15:18

❦

Thought for the Day

The trouble is not on the outside; it is in the inner recesses of a person's being.

Harold Fickett

Matthew 15:1-31
Proverbs 26:24-26

Date _____

WEEK 4 / *Wednesday*

Verse of the Day

Simon Peter answered, "You are the Christ, the Son of the living God."

Matthew 16:16

❦

Thought for the Day

Take care that you do not become content with getting his help; love him for himself.

F. B. Meyer

Matthew 15:32-16:20

Isaiah 55:1-2

WEEK 4 / Thursday   Date _____

Verse of the Day

"If people want to follow me, they must give up the things they want."

Matthew 16:24

Thought for the Day

Christ's love so wishes our joy that it is ruthless against everything in us that diminishes our joy.

Frederick Buechner

Matthew 16:21-17:13

Isaiah 53:6-10

Date _____

WEEK 4 / Friday

Verse of the Day

"The greatest person in the kingdom of heaven is the one who makes himself humble like this child."

Matthew 18:4

❦

Thought for the Day

God seeks and loves courageous souls. But they must be humble and have no confidence in themselves.

St. Teresa of Avila

Matthew 7:14-18:9

2 Chronicles 33: 12-13

Week 4 / Weekend

Date _____

Verse of the Day

"You must forgive him even if he does wrong to you seventy-seven times."

Matthew 18:22b

Thought for the Day

The rush of God's strength, which brings forgiveness, gives in turn the ability to forgive... and to forgive.

David Augsburger

Matthew 18:10-35
Ezekiel 18:21-23

Date _____

WEEK 5 / *Monday*

Verse of the Day

"God can do all things."

Matthew 19:26

🍂

Thought for the Day

Jesus supplies the power to change the human heart.

F. F. Bruce

Matthew 19:1-26

Malachi 2:13-16

WEEK 5 / Tuesday

Date _____

Verse of the Day

"Are you jealous because I am good to those people?"

Matthew 20:15b

❦

Thought for the Day

The revolution of God is a leveling revolution.

David Wenham

Matthew 19:27-20:19

1 Samuel 2:2, 6-8b

Date _____

WEEK 5 / Wednesday

Verse of the Day

"The Son of Man did not come to be served. He came to serve others and to give his life as a ransom for many people.

Matthew 20:28

❦

Thought for the Day

Jesus smiles and quietly reassures us, "My Father will honor the one who serves me."

F. LaGard Smith

Matthew 20:20-21:11

Psalm 95:1-3

WEEK 5 / Thursday

Date _____

Verse of the Day

"If you believe, you will get anything you ask for in prayer."

Matthew 21:22

❦

Thought for the Day

We go to worship in praise and thank God for what he has done, is doing, and will do.

Robert Webber

Matthew 21:12-32

Psalm 26:8

Date _____

WEEK 5 / Friday

Verse of the Day

"Yes, many people are invited, but only a few are chosen."

Matthew 22:14

Thought for the Day

Who can become a Christian? Anyone can, because God's grace closes nobody out.

Clark Pinnock

Matthew 21:33-22:14

Isaiah 56:3-5

Week 5 / Weekend

Date _____

Verse of the Day

"Give to Caesar the things that are Caesar's, and give to God the things that are God's."

Matthew 22:21

❧

Thought for the Day

I have placed my neck in other worldly nooses and yokes, but only the yoke of Christ grants me freedom.

Jeanie Miley

Matthew 22:15-40

Deuteronomy 6: 4-9

Date _____

WEEK 6 / Monday

Verse of the Day

"Whoever makes himself humble will be made great."

Matthew 23:12b

🍎

Thought for the Day

American evangelicalism is awash in a theology that wouldn't empower a clockwork mouse, let alone a disciple of Christ.

Os Guinness

Matthew 22:41-23:22

Jeremiah 5:30-31

WEEK 6 / Tuesday   Date _____

Verse of the Day

"Be careful that no one fools you. Many will come in my name, saying, 'I am the Christ.'"

Matthew 24:4-5

Thought for the Day

If you live the out-and-out Christian life, the world will soon give *you* up.

J. Sydlow Baxter of D. L. Moody

Matthew 23:23-24:8

Psalm 94:20-23

Date _____

WEEK 6 / Wednesday

Verse of the Day

"But those people who keep their faith until the end will be saved."

Matthew 24:13

❦

Thought for the Day

Many of the signs Jesus said would herald His return have developed before our eyes.

J. Oswald Sanders

Matthew 24:9-35

Isaiah 13:9-10

WEEK 6 / Thursday

Date _____

Verse of the Day

"So always be ready, because you don't know the day or the hour the Son of Man will come."

Matthew 25:13

❧

Thought for the Day

He is coming again and we yet have time to trust in Him as our Savior and Lord.

Billy Graham

Matthew 24:36-25:13

Malachi 3:1, 2, 5, 16-18

Date _____

WEEK 6 / Friday

Verse of the Day

"I tell you the truth, anything you did for even the least of my people here, you also did for me."

Matthew 25:40

❦

Thought for the Day

Imagine the impact Christians could have on the world if kindness were the rule in all we do!

Bill Bright

Matthew 25:14-40

Psalm 41:1-3

WEEK 6 / *Weekend* Date _____

Verse of the Day

A woman approached him with an alabaster jar filled with expensive perfume. She poured this perfume on Jesus' head while he was eating.

Matthew 26:7

Thought for the Day

Higher than our own comfort or success should be the one thought of the glory of our God.

F. B. Meyer

Matthew 25:41-26:19

Judges 13:15-23

Date _____

WEEK 7 / Monday

Verse of the Day

This blood is poured out for many to forgive their sins.

Matthew 26:28b

Thought for the Day

How gently did He gather me to Himself, to His truth, to His blood, to His love.

Charles Spurgeon

Matthew 26:20-46

Ezekiel 34:11-12, 16a

WEEK 7 / Tuesday

Date _____

Verse of the Day

At once Judas went to Jesus and said, "Greetings, Teacher!" and kissed him.

Matthew 26:49

❦

Thought for the Day

Do we believe in Jesus, yet live our lives as if we didn't? Will today be a day of betrayal?

F. LaGard Smith

Matthew 26:47-68
Psalm 55:12-14, 20-21

Date _____

WEEK 7 / Wednesday

Verse of the Day

"Don't do anything to that man, because he is innocent."

Matthew 27:19b

❦

Thought for the Day

Oh, the madness of committing sin in the immediate presence of a Majesty so great.

St. Teresa of Avila

Matthew 26:69-27:20

Daniel 2:26-28a

WEEK 7 / Thursday

Date _____

Verse of the Day

When the soldiers had crucified him, they threw lots to decide who would get his clothes.

Matthew 27:35

❦

Thought for the Day

Let us depend on God's Holy Spirit for the wisdom and strength required to respond to mistreatment.

Bill Bright

Matthew 27:21-44
Isaiah 53:1-3, 5

Date _____

WEEK 7 / Friday

Verse of the Day

He is risen from the dead as he said he would.

Matthew 28:6b

❦

Thought for the Day

Resurrection is not just a passport to heaven, but a power to change us now.

Lloyd Ogilvie

Matthew 27:45-28:10

Psalm 16:8-10

Week 7 / Weekend

Date _____

Verse of the Day

Then Jesus came to them and said, "All power in heaven and on earth is given to me."

Matthew 28:18

❦

Thought for the Day

The gospel is not theology. It's a Person. Theology doesn't save. Jesus Christ saves.

Richard Halverson

Matthew 28:11-Mark 1:20

1 Chronicles 16:23-25

Date _____

WEEK 8 / Monday

Verse of the Day

Immediately the disease left the man, and he was healed.

Mark 1:42

❦

Thought for the Day

He is the broken, and He is the healer.

Gloria Gaither

Mark 1:21-45
Hosea 6:1-3

WEEK 8 / Tuesday

Date _____

Verse of the Day

"I will prove to you that the Son of Man has authority on earth to forgive sins."

Mark 2:10

Thought for the Day

The believer can never forget, either here or in eternity, that he is a forgiven sinner.

Andrew Murray

Mark 2:1-22
Isaiah 53:10-12

Date _____

WEEK 8 / Wednesday

Verse of the Day

"The Sabbath day was made to help people..."

Mark 2:27

❦

Thought for the Day

Sabbath means a rest that brings peace into the private world.

Gordon MacDonald

Mark 2:23-3:27

Isaiah 56:1-2

WEEK 8 / Thursday

Date _____

Verse of the Day

"My true brother and sister and mother are those who do what God wants."

Mark 3:35

Thought for the Day

No one who is disobedient to God can have confidence in Him. Confidence is a result of obedience.

G. Steinberger

Mark 3:28-4:20

Exodus 19:3-5

Date _____

WEEK 8 / Friday

Verse of the Day

"Do you hide a lamp under a bowl or under a bed? No! You put the lamp on a lamp stand."

Mark 4:21

❦

Thought for the Day

At the cross the penalty for sin was paid; the justice of God was satisfied.

Richard Foster

Mark 4:21-5:10
Pslam 29:3-5, 7, 10

Week 8 / Weekend

Date _____

Verse of the Day

"Dear woman, you are made well because you believed. Go in peace; be healed of your disease."

Mark 5:34

❦

Thought for the Day

It is by faith that we stand, by resolutions we fall.

Charles Finney

Mark 5:11-36

1 Samuel 17: 42-27, 50

Date _____

WEEK 9 / Monday

Verse of the Day

So the followers went out and preached that people should change their hearts and lives.

Mark 6:12

🍎

Thought for the Day

Christians do not fight for victory; we fight from victory.

Warren Wiersbe

Mark 5:37-6:20

Deuteronomy 1: 42-45

Week 9 / Tuesday

Date _____

Verse of the Day

"Come away by yourselves, and we will go to a lonely place to get some rest."

Mark 6:31b

Thought for the Day

When you feel so absorbed in God's interests that you are indifferent to your own, all becomes clear.

F. B. Meyer

Mark 6:21-44
Psalm 107:8-9

Date _____

WEEK 9 / Wednesday

Verse of the Day

"Have courage! It is I. Do not be afraid."

Mark 6:50b

Thought for the Day

We are called to be a channel of divine mercy flowing through us to others.

Lloyd Ogilvie

Mark 6:45-7:13
Pslam 78:32-39

WEEK 9 / Thursday

Date _____

Verse of the Day

"There is nothing people put into their bodies that makes them unclean. People are made unclean by the things that come out of them."

Mark 7:15

Thought for the Day

A Christian's good character is the character of Jesus breathed into each of us by the Holy Spirit.

Patrick Morley

Mark 7:14-37
Proverbs 6:12-19

Date _____

WEEK 9 / Friday

Verse of the Day

Jesus sighed deeply and said, "Why do you people ask for a miracle as a sign?"

Mark 8:12

❦

Thought for the Day

Judas heard the gospel according to Jesus, yet he refused to turn from his sin and selfishness.

John F. MacArthur, Jr.

Mark 8:1-26
Psalm 78:40-43

WEEK 9 / *Weekend*

Date _____

Verse of the Day

"If people want to follow me, they must give up the things they want."

Mark 8:34

Thought for the Day

Renounce therefore all things, and labor to please your Creator.

Thomas a Kempis

Mark 8:27-9:13
Ecclesiastes 2:10-11

Date _____

WEEK 10 / Monday

Verse of the Day

"Whoever wants to be the most important must be last of all and servant of all."

Mark 9:35

Thought for the Day

We may count on Him to teach us His way and show us His path not only in special trials and hard times, but in everyday life.

Andrew Murray

Mark 9:14-37
Exodus 33:7-11

Week 10 / Tuesday

Date _____

Verse of the Day

"Whoever is not against us is with us."

Mark 9:40

❦

Thought for the Day

Repentance is a matter neither of emotion nor of speech. It is an inward change of mind.

John Stott

Mark 9:38-10:16
Genesis 39:6b-12

Date _____

Week 10 / Wednesday

Verse of the Day

"Many who have the highest place now will have the lowest place in the future."

Mark 10:31

❣

Thought for the Day

Write, read, chant, mourn, keep silence, pray, endure crosses manfully. Life everlasting is worth all these.

Thomas a Kempis

Mark 10:17-41

Psalm 58:11

WEEK 10 / Thursday

Date _____

Verse of the Day

"In the same way, the Son of Man did not come to be served. He came to serve others and to give his life as a ransom for many people."

Mark 10:45

❦

Thought for the Day

The Cross is the best evidence that there is much more to love than justice, much more to right than rights.

Thomas Schmidt

Mark 10:42-11:14

Genesis 22:1-2, 10-12

Date _____

WEEK 10 / Friday

Verse of the Day

I tell you the truth, you can say to this mountain, 'Go, fall into the sea.' And if you have no doubts in your mind and believe that what you say will happen, God will do it for you.

Mark 11:23

Thought for the Day

Don't spend time describing your mountain to the Lord. He knows what it is. Instead, focus your attention on the mountain mover.

Bill Hybels

Mark 11:15-12:12
Psalm 145:18-19

WEEK 10 / *Weekend*

Date _____

Verse of the Day

"Love the Lord your God with all your heart, all your soul, all your mind, and all your strength."

Mark 12:30

Thought for the Day

Persecution is to the Christian what "growing pains" are to a child.

Billy Graham

Mark 12:13-31

Psalm 140:1-8

Date _____

WEEK 11 / Monday

Verse of the Day

"This woman is very poor, but she gave all she had; she gave all she had to live on."

Mark 12:44

❦

Thought for the Day

God condescends to use us; and as we give, He is pleased to entrust to us more and more.

George Muller

Mark 12:32-13:10
Exodus 36:3b-7

Week 11 / Tuesday

Date _____

Verse of the Day

Then people will see the Son of Man coming in clouds with great power and glory.

Mark 13:26

Thought for the Day

On Christ the solid Rock, I stand; All other ground is sinking sand.

Edward Mote

Mark 13:11-37
Daniel 11:33-35

Date _____

WEEK 11 / Wednesday

Verse of the Day

Then Jesus said, "This is my blood which is the new agreement that God makes with his people."

Mark 14:24

❦

Thought for the Day

The death and resurrection of Jesus Christ reaches down through history and becomes a present reality to the people who celebrate it in faith.

Robert Webber

Mark 14:1-26

Exodus 12:14, 25-27

Week 11 / Thursday

Date _____

Verse of the Day

Jesus answered, "I tell you the truth, tonight before the rooster crows twice you will say three times you don't know me."

Mark 14:30

Thought for the Day

Like a song unending, the words keep singing... I am totally forgiven, I am continually cleansed, just for Jesus' sake.

Ruth Calkin

Mark 14:27-52
1 Kings 8:54-59

Date _____

WEEK 11 / Friday

Verse of the Day

"... you will see the Son of Man sitting at the right hand of God, the Powerful One, and coming on clouds in the sky."

Mark 14:62

❦

Thought for the Day

Commit your right and your honor into God's keeping.

Andrew Murray

Mark 14:53-15:5

Psalm 26:1-2

Week 11 / Weekend

Date _____

Verse of the Day

The soldiers crucified Jesus and divided his clothes among themselves..."

Mark 15:24

❧

Thought for the Day

And so, long before we ever thought of God, we were in His thoughts.

D. L. Moody

Mark 15:6-32
Psalm 22:16-18

Date _____

WEEK 12 / Monday

Verse of the Day

Then the women looked and saw that the stone had already been rolled away, even though it was very large.

Mark 16:4

❦

Thought for the Day

At the cross we see His love, but in resurrection we see His power.

John G. Mitchell

Mark 15:33-16:8
Isaiah 35:7-10

WEEK 12 / Tuesday

Date _____

Verse of the Day

Jesus said to his followers, "Go everywhere in the world, and tell the Good News to everyone."

Mark 16:15

❦

Thought for the Day

The Bible says there will be a day of reckoning to those who spurned His love.

Bill Hybels

Mark 16:9-Luke 1:13

Numbers 14:6-7, 9, 11, 20-24

Date _____

WEEK 12 / *Wednesday*

Verse of the Day

"You are blessed because you believed that what the Lord said to you would really happen."

Luke 1:45

❦

Thought for the Day

Believers, look up – take courage. The angels are nearer than you think.

Billy Graham

Luke 1:14-45

Malachi 4:5-6

Week 12 / Thursday

Date _____

Verse of the Day

He has helped his servant, the people of Israel, remembering to show them mercy.

Luke 1:54

❧

Thought for the Day

He may discipline us, but in His mercy, He will never forsake us.

William Stoddard

Luke 1:46-77

Lamentations 3: 21-26

Date _____

WEEK 12 / Friday

Verse of the Day

Today your Savior was born in the town of David.

Luke 2:11

Thought for the Day

God came in Christ to pay the full price, and at the cross, exposed His heart.

Lloyd Ogilvie

Luke 1:78-2:26

Isaiah 12:2b-5a

WEEK 12 / Weekend

Date _____

Verse of the Day

"Why were you looking for me? Didn't you know that I must be in my Father's house?"

Luke 2:49

Thought for the Day

God's all-stars, are not people of ability; they are people of availability.

James Merritt

Luke 2:27-52
1 Samuel 1:24-28

Date _____

WEEK 13 / Monday

Verse of the Day

"And all the people will know about the salvation of God!"

Luke 3:6

❧

Thought for the Day

Remain balanced, cheerful, winsome, and stable, anticipating His return day by day.

Charles Swindoll

Luke 3:1-22

Isaiah 40:6, 8, 9c-10

WEEK 13 / Tuesday

Date _____

Verse of the Day

When Jesus began his ministry, he was about thirty years old.

Luke 3:23

🍎

Thought for the Day

God, in a marvelous way, defeated the evil tactics of the devil, thereby fulfilling the promise of giving a light forever.

Herbert Lockyer

Luke 3:23-38
Isaiah 11:1-5

Date _____

WEEK 13 / Wednesday

Verse of the Day

God sent me to free those who have been treated unfairly.

Luke 4:18

❦

Thought for the Day

The mission of the Incarnate One was to free the oppressed.

Ronald Sider

Luke 4:1-30

Isaiah 61:1-3a

WEEK 13 / Thursday

Date _____

Verse of the Day

They were amazed at his teaching, because he spoke with authority.

Luke 4:32

Thought for the Day

The secret of spiritual happiness and blessing is simply trusting and obeying the Lord.

David Reid

Luke 4:31-5:11

2 Kings 5:10-11a, 13-14

Date _____

WEEK 13 / Friday

Verse of the Day

Jesus said to him, "Follow me." So Levi got up, left everything, and followed him.

Luke 5:27-28

❦

Thought for the Day

For he who was love incarnate had his own needs to love and be loved.

Margaret Magdalen

Luke 5:12-35

Psalm 119: 145-151

Week 13 / Weekend

Date _____

Verse of the Day

You people who are poor are happy, because the kingdom of God belongs to you.

Luke 6:20

Thought for the Day

We see the manifestations of ineffable bliss in their souls.

Charles Finney

Luke 5:36-6:23

Psalm 37:10-13

Date _____

WEEK 14 / Monday

Verse of the Day

Do to others what you would want them to do to you.

Luke 6:31

🍎

Thought for the Day

God promises that those who reach out and demonstrate mercy will, in turn, receive it . . .

Charles Swindoll

Luke 6:24-45
Jonah 4:1-2

Week 14 / Tuesday

Date _____

Verse of the Day

"Why do you call me, 'Lord, Lord,' but do not do what I say?"

Luke 6:46

Thought for the Day

Why be less sensible in building a character than in building a house?

Joseph Parker

Luke 6:46-7:23
Psalm 18:46

Date _____

WEEK 14 / Wednesday

Verse of the Day

Jesus said to the woman, "Because you believed, you are saved from your sins. Go in peace."

Luke 7:50

Thought for the Day

We cannot be satisfied with our goodness after beholding the holiness of God.

Billy Graham

Luke 7:24-50

Job 11:4-6

WEEK 14 / Thursday

Date _____

Verse of the Day

Jesus answered them, "My mother and my brothers are those who listen to God's teaching and obey it!"

Luke 8:21

Thought for the Day

Sin leads to a rejection of God and God's truth, and the rejection of God's truth leads to even greater sin.

James Boice

Luke 8:1-21
Psalm 78:1-4

Date _____

WEEK 14 / Friday

Verse of the Day

But Jesus said, "Someone did touch me, because I felt power go out from me."

Luke 8:46

Thought for the Day

Jesus' followers are not insulated from the tragedies of this world, just as He was not.

Philip Yancey

Luke 8:22-48

Psalm 9:9

Week 14 / Weekend

Date _____

Verse of the Day

They all ate and were satisfied . . .

Luke 9:17

Thought for the Day

Our Father watches over His children, quietly overseeing the events of their lives . . .

Phillip Keller

Luke 8:49-9:17

Job 12:7-10

Date _____

WEEK 15 / Monday

Verse of the Day

A voice came from the cloud, saying, "This is my Son, whom I have chosen. Listen to him!"

Luke 9:35

❦

Thought for the Day

If God required perfection before He admitted us into the circle of His fellowship, who would qualify?

J. Oswald Sanders

Luke 9:18-43a
Nehemiah 9:30-31

WEEK 15 / Tuesday   Date _____

Verse of the Day

So pray to God, who owns the harvest, that he will send more workers to help gather his harvest.

Luke 10:2b

Thought for the Day

That is the peril of prayer... As we begin to talk to God and hear him speak to us, life may never be the same.

Bruce Larson

Luke 9:43b-10:7

2 Chronicles 16: 7-9b

Date _____

WEEK 15 / Wednesday

Verse of the Day

But you should not be happy because the spirits obey you but because your names are written in heaven.

Luke 10:20

❦

Thought for the Day

People give up before they have prevailed, and hence, the enduement of spiritual power is not received.

Charles Finney

Luke 10:8-29
1 Kings 4:29-34

Week 15 / Thursday

Date _____

Verse of the Day

Forgive us our sins, because we forgive everyone who has done wrong to us.

Luke 11:4

❦

Thought for the Day

We need to develop a kind disposition, to be sensitive to others and truly desire their happiness.

Jerry Bridges

Luke 10:30-11:13
Proverbs 3:27-28

Date _____

WEEK 15 / Friday

Verse of the Day

When your eyes are good, your whole body will be full of light.

Luke 11:34b

Thought for the Day

You cannot hide Christ if once He comes within. If the light is there, it simply must shine.

G. Campbell Morgan

Luke 11:14-36
Proverbs 4:25-27

WEEK 15 / Weekend

Date _____

Verse of the Day

Fear the one who has the power to kill you and also to throw you into hell. Yes, this is the one you should fear.

Luke 12:5b

Thought for the Day

The fear of the Lord is to love what God loves and to hate what God hates.

Patrick Morley

Luke 11:37-12:7
Isaiah 51:12-13a

Date _____

WEEK 16 / Monday

Verse of the Day

Be careful and guard against all kinds of greed.

Luke 12:15

❦

Thought for the Day

Wherever you find the treasure, you will find the heart.

Richard Foster

Luke 12:8-34

Ecclesiastes 5:10-11

WEEK 16 / Tuesday

Date _____

Verse of the Day

Be dressed, ready for service, and have your lamps shining.

Luke 12:35

Thought for the Day

The faithful ones can confidently expect to be rewarded for their faithfulness . . .

Al Bryant

Luke 12:35-56

Psalm 24:1-6

Date _____

WEEK 16 / Wednesday

Verse of the Day

... but the entire crowd rejoiced at all the wonderful things Jesus was doing.

Luke 13:17b

Thought for the Day

Amid all who surround him, he becomes like a tree of life, of which they can taste and be refreshed.

Andrew Murray

Luke 12:57-13:21
Isaiah 5:7, 15-16

WEEK 16 / Thursday

Date _____

Verse of the Day

... but those who make themselves humble will be made great.

Luke 14:11b

❦

Thought for the Day

Pride is not the answer to the human problem; it is the human problem.

Sherwood Wirt

Luke 13:22-14:14
Proverbs 18:12

Date _____

WEEK 16 / Friday

Verse of the Day

... there is joy in the presence of the angels of God when one sinner changes his heart and life.

Luke 15:10

Thought for the Day

He offers no cheap grace. No easy life. "Salvation is free, but not cheap."

Billy Graham

Luke 14:15-15:10

Daniel 3:16-18

WEEK 16 / Weekend

Date _____

Verse of the Day

We had to celebrate and be happy because your brother was dead, but now he is alive.

Luke 15:32

Thought for the Day

Until the heart is voluntarily opened up, the process of rebuilding a broken world cannot begin . . .

Gordon MacDonald

Luke 15:11-16:18
Ezekiel 33:15

Date _____

WEEK 17 / Monday

Verse of the Day

God knows what is really in your hearts.

Luke 16:15

Thought for the Day

With God, life is not a guessing game. His judgments are sure.

Elliot Johnson/ Al Scheirbaum

Luke 16:9-17:4
Psalm 139:23-24

WEEK 17 / Tuesday

Date _____

Verse of the Day

When the Son of Man comes again, he will shine like lightning, which flashes across the sky...

Luke 17:24

❦

Thought for the Day

There will be a day of reckoning when God closes His books on time and judges every creature...

Billy Graham

Luke 17:5-37
Genesis 19:12-13

Date _____

WEEK 17 / Wednesday

Verse of the Day

The Lord said, "Listen to what the unfair judge said. God will always give what is right to his people...

Luke 18:6-7

Thought for the Day

We can share because we know that he will care for us...

Richard Foster

Luke 18:1-25
Jeremiah 9:23-24a

WEEK 17 / Thursday

Date _____

Verse of the Day

The Son of Man came to find lost people and save them.

Luke 19:10

Thought for the Day

If we want to have victory over sin, then we must see our sin from God's perspective.

Floyd McClung

Luke 18:26-19:10
Jonah 3:4-5, 10

Date _____

WEEK 17 / Friday

Verse of the Day

God bless the king who comes in the name of the Lord!

Luke 19:38
(Psalm 118:26)

❦

Thought for the Day

Reward or loss signify an enriched or impoverished relationship with God...

J. I. Packer

Luke 19:11-40
Isaiah 3:10-11

Week 17 / Weekend

Date _____

Verse of the Day

"I wish you knew today what would bring you peace."

Luke 19:42

Thought for the Day

Jesus did not come to change Israel's politics, He came to change men's hearts.

Warren Wiersbe

Luke 19:41-20:19

Isaiah 1:10, 15b-16

Date _____

WEEK 18 / Monday

Verse of the Day

Jesus said to them, "Then give to Caesar the things that are Caesar's, and give to God the things that are God's."

Luke 20:25

🍎

Thought for the Day

Do you see the importance of praying continually for a quick and tender and powerful conscience?

Charles Finney

Luke 20:20-47
Micah 2:1-3

WEEK 18 / Tuesday

Date _____

Verse of the Day

By continuing to have faith you will save your lives.

Luke 21:19

Thought for the Day

Rely upon the fact that God is the source of your thoughts and words.

H. Norman Wright

Luke 21:1-28

Exodus 4:10-11, 14-15

Date _____

WEEK 18 / Wednesday

Verse of the Day

Earth and sky will be destroyed, but the words I have spoken will never be destroyed.

Luke 21:33

❦

Thought for the Day

As long as we do not have this Hope, we are really without hope.

G. Steinberger

Luke 21:29-22:20

Psalm 119:57-60

Week 18 / Thursday

Date _____

Verse of the Day

Just as my Father has given me a kingdom, I also give you a kingdom.

Luke 22:29a

Thought for the Day

I ask God in prayer to reveal His will to me aright.

George Muller

Luke 22:21-53
Psalm 143:9-10

Date _____

Week 18 / Friday

Verse of the Day

Then Peter went outside and cried painfully.

Luke 22:62

Thought for the Day

A broken truth often means a broken heart.

R. C. Sproul

Luke 22:54-23:12

Genesis 27:35-37, 41

WEEK 18 / Weekend

Date _____

Verse of the Day

Jesus said, "Father, forgive them, because they don't know what they are doing."

Luke 23:34

❧

Thought for the Day

Corrie ten Boom challenged prisoners that they could accept or reject Christ and His forgiveness.

Ruth Tucker

Luke 23:13-43
Isaiah 30:15, 18

Date _____

WEEK 19 / Monday

Verse of the Day

Jesus cried out in a loud voice, "Father, I give you my life." After Jesus said this, he died.

Luke 23:46

❦

Thought for the Day

The ground trembled, and the rock of the tomb tumbled. And the flower of Easter blossomed.

Max Lucado

Luke 23:44-24:12
Isaiah 42:1-4, 6-7b

WEEK 19 / Tuesday

Date _____

Verse of the Day

"The Lord really has risen from the dead!"

Luke 24:34

Thought for the Day

The whole life of every believer is to be a proclamation of the glad tidings.

Charles Finney

Luke 24:13-53

Isaiah 40:9-10a

Date _____

WEEK 19 / Wednesday

Verse of the Day

In the beginning there was the Word. The Word was with God, and the Word was God.

John 1:1

❦

Thought for the Day

The truth of the Incarnation remains intact and inviolate . . .

Malcolm Muggeridge

John 1:1-28
Isaiah 9:2, 6

WEEK 19 / Thursday

Date _____

Verse of the Day

"Look, the Lamb of God, who takes away the sin of the world!"

John 1:29

❦

Thought for the Day

He bled, and died, and I have been transfused.

Luci Shaw

John 1:29-51
Isaiah 53:6-8

Date _____

WEEK 19 / Friday

Verse of the Day

Jesus answered them, "Destroy this temple, and I will build it again in three days."

John 2:19

❦

Thought for the Day

Christ cleansed the temple when men sinned and made it unclean.

John G. Mitchell

John 2:1-25
Psalm 101:6-8

WEEK 19 / Weekend

Date _____

Verse of the Day

... unless one is born again, he cannot be in God's kingdom.

John 3:3

❧

Thought for the Day

God loves us as individuals He knows by name.

Lucille Sollenberger

John 3:1-30
Isaiah 59:15b-17

Date _____

WEEK 20 / Monday

Verse of the Day

Those who believe in the Son have eternal life, but those who do not obey the Son will never have life.

John 3:36

❧

Thought for the Day

Our spirits can only find life in the Living Spirit of the Living Lord.

W. Phillip Keller

John 3:31-4:26

Jeremiah 2:12-13, 18-19

Week 20 / Tuesday

Date _____

Verse of the Day

Jesus said, "My food is to do what the One who sent me wants me to do..."

John 4:34

Thought for the Day

Mountain-moving faith will be given to us as we step out and follow the Lord's direction.

Bill Hybels

John 4:27-54

2 Chronicles 20: 20-22

Date _____

WEEK 20 / Wednesday

Verse of the Day

Then Jesus said, "Stand up. Pick up your mat and walk."

John 5:8

❧

Thought for the Day

The Bible says that man, in his natural condition, is "dead to God" and action of the Holy Spirit is required.

Terry Fullam

John 5:1-29
Psalm 34:21-22

WEEK 20 / Thursday

Date _____

Verse of the Day

I tell you this so you can be saved.

John 5:34b

❦

Thought for the Day

The only thing more absurd than the gift is our stubborn unwillingness to receive it.

Max Lucado

John 5:30-6:15
Genesis 49:9-10

Date _____

WEEK 20 / Friday

Verse of the Day

Jesus answered, "The work God wants you to do is this: Believe the One he sent."

John 6:29

Thought for the Day

Children are a poignant reminder of simple trust and what faith is all about.

Ruth Senter

John 6:16-40

1 Chronicles 16: 8-12

WEEK 20 / Weekend

Date _____

Verse of the Day

I tell you the truth, whoever believes has eternal life.

John 6:47

❧

Thought for the Day

Our help is to come from Him as we run into the shelter of His arms.

Edith Schaeffer

John 6:41-71

Numbers 14:1-4

Date _____

WEEK 21 / Monday

Verse of the Day

But I know him, because I am from him, and he sent me.

John 7:29

❦

Thought for the Day

No man was ever more loving than Jesus Christ.

R. C. Sproul

John 7:1-31
1 Kings 22:7-8

Week 21 / Tuesday

Date _____

Verse of the Day

"Let anyone who is thirsty come to me and drink."

John 7:37b

Thought for the Day

Salvation is offered by divine grace, not by human works.

Charles Swindoll

John 7:32-8:11

Proverbs 20:9

Date _____

WEEK 21 / Wednesday

Verse of the Day

"I am the light of the world. The person who follows me will never live in darkness..."

John 8:12b

❦

Thought for the Day

Christ was the revelation of the Father on earth.

Andrew Murray

John 8:12-41

Psalm 2:10-12

Week 21 / Thursday

Date _____

Verse of the Day

The person who belongs to God accepts what God says.

John 8:47a

Thought for the Day

If you want to know the way, let us again study Jesus.

Andrew Murray

John 8:42-9:12

Numbers 25:10-12

Date _____

WEEK 21 / Friday

Verse of the Day

"I don't know if he is a sinner. One thing I do know: I was blind, and now I see."

John 9:25

Thought for the Day

To follow him means not to walk in darkness.

John G. Mitchell

John 9:13-41
Psalm 119:17-24

Week 21 / Weekend

Date _____

Verse of the Day

"I am the door, and the person who enters through me will be saved."

John 10:9

❦

Thought for the Day

He would not lead us into a dark valley He was not prepared to overcome.

F. B. Meyer

John 10:1-33
Isaiah 40:11

Date _____

WEEK 22 / Monday

Verse of the Day

Martha answered, "Yes, Lord, I believe that you are the Christ, the Son of God..."

John 11:27

❦

Thought for the Day

God never wearies of holding the rope. We can confidently leave it in His strong hand.

Millie Stamm

John 10:34-11:27

Psalm 40:1-3

Week 22 / Tuesday

Date _____

Verse of the Day

Jesus cried. So the Jews said, "See how much he loved him."

John 11:35-36

❦

Thought for the Day

Martha needed only the faith to give orders to move the stone. Lazarus was raised from the dead.

John White

John 11:28-57

1 Kings 17: 21-22, 24

Date _____

WEEK 22 / Wednesday

Verse of the Day

She poured the perfume on Jesus' feet, and then she wiped his feet with her hair.

John 12:3b

Thought for the Day

The next pity party we are tempted to throw for ourselves, we must remember, we are not alone.

Charles Swindoll

John 12:1-26
Psalm 10:12-15

Week 22 / Thursday

Date _____

Verse of the Day

If I am lifted up from the earth, I will draw all people toward me.

John 12:32

❦

Thought for the Day

"There is no wickedness like the wickedness of unbelief."

C. H. Spurgeon of Dr. Heugh

John 12:27-13:5

Numbers 11:10-11, 13b-16a, 21-23

Date _____

WEEK 22 / Friday

Verse of the Day

"If I, your Lord and Teacher, have washed your feet, you also should wash each other's feet."

John 13:14

Thought for the Day

The churches that obey our Lord's command to "love one another" usually are filled to overflowing . . .

Bill Bright

John 13:6-35
Exodus 20:3, 5a, 7a, 8, 12a, 13-17a

Week 22 / Weekend

Date _____

Verse of the Day

Jesus said, "Don't let your hearts be troubled. Trust in God, and trust in me."

John 14:1

Thought for the Day

The perfect happiness of perfect obedience will dawn upon your soul . . .

Hannah Whitall Smith

John 13:36-14:26

Deuteronomy 11: 13-14

Date _____

WEEK 23 / *Monday*

Verse of the Day

Don't let your hearts be troubled or afraid.

John 14:27b

❦

Thought for the Day

Religion is meant to be in everyday life a thing of unspeakable joy.

Andrew Murray

John 14:27-15:27

Psalm 51:10-13

WEEK 23 / Tuesday

Date _____

Verse of the Day

But I tell you the truth, it is better for you that I go away. When I go away, I will send the Helper to you.

John 16:7

Thought for the Day

Stand still, whisper his name, and listen. He is nearer than you think.

Max Lucado

John 16:1-28
Psalm 37:3-6

Date _____

WEEK 23 / Wednesday

Verse of the Day

In this world you will have trouble, but be brave! I have defeated the world!

John 16:33b

❦

Thought for the Day

Our security is in clinging to a God who takes care of those who take the conscious step of faith to believe.

Joel Gregory

John 16:29-17:20

Psalm 91:1-8

WEEK 23 / Thursday

Date _____

Verse of the Day

As you are in me and I am in you, I pray that they can also be one in us.

John 17:21

Thought for the Day

As God's people, we must overcome disunity before we can fight any other battles.

Anthony Evans

John 17:21-18:18
Psalm 133:1-3

Date _____

Week 23 / Friday

Verse of the Day

Jesus answered, "My kingdom does not belong to this world."

John 18:36

Thought for the Day

Pilot judged the Truth.
He sentenced the Truth.
He scourged the Truth.
He crucified the Truth.

R. C. Sproul

John 18:19-19:3
Psalm 117:1-2

Week 23 / Weekend

Date _____

Verse of the Day

Jesus answered, "The only power you have over me is the power given to you by God."

John 19:11

Thought for the Day

Despite the suffering, violence, and filth of the world, God remains in control.

Elliot Johnson/ Al Schierbaum

John 19:4-27
Jeremiah 27:4-7

Date _____

WEEK 24 / Monday

Verse of the Day

"They have taken the Lord out of the tomb, and we don't know where they have put him."

John 20:2

💚

Thought for the Day

Christ is risen: The angels of God are rejoicing. Christ is risen: The tombs of the dead are empty.

Hippolytus of Rome

John 19:28-20:9
Psalm 47:1-9

WEEK 24 / Tuesday

Date _____

Verse of the Day

Then Jesus said, "Peace be with you. As the Father sent me I now send you."

John 20:21

Thought for the Day

Put your powerlessness in God's almighty power, and find in waiting on God your deliverance.

Andrew Murray

John 20:10-21:3

Judges 6:36-40

Date _____

WEEK 24 / Wednesday

Verse of the Day

Jesus said, "Take care of my sheep."

John 21:16b

❧

Thought for the Day

Our Good Shepherd loves to see His sheep contented and relaxed, refreshed and satisfied with Him.

Millie Stamm

John 21:4-25
Numbers 27:15-17

WEEK 24 / Thursday

Date _____

Verse of the Day

You will be my witnesses – in Jerusalem, in all of Judea, in Samaria, and in every part of the world."

Acts 1:8

❦

Thought for the Day

Since this is the day of salvation, we must be diligent to do all we can to win the lost.

Warren Wiersbe

Acts 1:1-26
Psalm 96:12-13

Date _____

WEEK 24 / Friday

Verse of the Day

They were all filled with the Holy Spirit, and they began to speak in different languages by the power the Holy Spirit was giving them.

Acts 2:4

❦

Thought for the Day

Without the Holy Spirit, we'll drift in irons and be lost at sea . . .

Lloyd Ogilvie

Acts 2:1-28
Isaiah 44:1-3

Week 24 / Weekend   Date _____

Verse of the Day

Peter said to them, "Change your hearts and lives and be baptized..."

Acts 2:38

❦

Thought for the Day

God looks for brokenness of spirit – for a contrite, humble heart...

Jill Briscoe

Acts 2:29-3:10

Hosea 6:1-3b

Date _____

WEEK 25 / Monday

Verse of the Day

It was faith in Jesus that made this crippled man well.

Acts 3:16

❦

Thought for the Day

We deserve to die for our sin, but Jesus died in our place.

James Boice

Acts 3:11-4:12

Isaiah 28:16-17

WEEK 25 / Tuesday

Date _____

Verse of the Day

We cannot keep quiet. We must speak about what we have seen and heard.

Acts 4:20

❦

Thought for the Day

People work is His work, and He will show us what to do, and even how to do it.

Jill Briscoe

Acts 4:13-37
Isaiah 43:4-7

Date _____

WEEK 25 / Wednesday

Verse of the Day

More and more men and women believed in the Lord and were added to the group of believers.

Acts 5:14

❦

Thought for the Day

We are in training now, learning bit by bit to manage money, power, time and temptation.

Lynn Anderson

Acts 5:1-26

Joshua 7:20-21, 24-25

Week 25 / Thursday

Date _____

Verse of the Day

We saw all these things happen. The Holy Spirit, whom God has given to all who obey him, also proves these things are true.

Acts 5:32

❦

Thought for the Day

He sees not only what He is doing, but what will come of what He is doing.

Charles Spurgeon

Acts 5:27-6:7
Isaiah 46:8-11

Date _____

WEEK 25 / Friday

Verse of the Day

Stephen was richly blessed by God who gave him the power to do great miracles...

Acts 6:8

🍎

Thought for the Day

When I am out of work I tell my Father. He is the best employment office.

Ruth Tucker

Acts 6:8-7:16

Psalm 105:1-4

Week 25 / Weekend

Date _____

Verse of the Day

He received commands from God that give life, and he gave those commands to us.

Acts 7:38b

Thought for the Day

All I have needed Thy hand hath provided. Great is Thy faithfulness, Lord, unto me!

Thomas O. Chisholm

Acts 7:17-42a
Psalm 105:28-37

Date _____

WEEK 26 / Monday

Verse of the Day

He said, "Look! I see heaven open and the Son of Man standing at God's right side."

Acts 7:56

Thought for the Day

When Stephen delivered his final, blistering denunciation, he did it with his eyes open.

J. Oswald Sanders

Acts 7:42b-8:1

2 Chronicles 24: 18-21

WEEK 26 / Tuesday

Date _____

Verse of the Day

And wherever they were scattered, they told people the Good News.

Acts 8:4

❧

Thought for the Day

Rejoice when another's success is greater than yours.

Marie Chapian

Acts 8:2-25

Numbers 16:1a, 2-3, 8-9, 28-30

Date _____

WEEK 26 / Wednesday

Verse of the Day

Philip began to speak, and starting with this same Scripture, he told the man the Good News about Jesus.

Acts 8:35

Thought for the Day

The Word of God is a constant and continuing source of joy for the Christian.

Al Bryant

Acts 8:26-9:9
Nehemiah 8:7-12

Week 26 / Thursday

Date _____

Verse of the Day

I will show him how much he must suffer for my name.

Acts 9:16

Thought for the Day

We feel that nothing can be wrongly ordered while He is the Director of our affairs . . .

Charles Spurgeon

Acts 9:10-35

1 Samuel 16: 12c-13

Date _____

WEEK 26 / Friday

Verse of the Day

The angel said, "God has heard your prayers."

Acts 10:4b

Thought for the Day

We pray to glorify God, but also to receive the benefits of prayer from His hand . . .

R. C. Sproul

Acts 9:36-10:23a
1 Kings 9:1-3

Week 26 / Weekend　　　Date _____

Verse of the Day

We saw what Jesus did in Judea and in Jerusalem, but the Jews in Jerusalem killed him by hanging him on a cross.

Acts 10:39

🍎

Thought for the Day

Without the cross the Discipline of confession would be only psychologically therapeutic.

Richard Foster

Acts 10:23b-48
Isaiah 1:18-20

Date _____

WEEK 27 / Monday

Verse of the Day

The Lord was helping the believers, and a large group of people believed and turned to the Lord.

Acts 11:21

❦

Thought for the Day

True compassion is an expression of the life of our Lord Jesus Christ.

William Fletcher

Acts 11:1-30

Proverbs 22:9

WEEK 27 / Tuesday

Date _____

Verse of the Day

He rescued me from Herod and all the things the Jewish people thought would happen.

Acts 12:11b

Thought for the Day

If God could deliver these men from the fiery furnace, it should seem evident He can deliver us from whatever troubles we find ourselves in . . .

Richard Lee

Acts 12:1-25
Exodus 14:29-31

Date _____

WEEK 27 / Wednesday

Verse of the Day

"Brothers, if you have any message that will encourage the people, please speak."

Acts 13:15b

Thought for the Day

God, who made the visible heaven and earth, does not disdain to work visible miracles . . .

St. Augustine

Acts 13:1-25
Exodus 4:29-31

WEEK 27 / Thursday

Date _____

Verse of the Day

But through Jesus everyone who believes is free from all sins.

Acts 13:39b

Thought for the Day

Enjoying God is really a vital expression of glorifying Him.

Lloyd Ogilvie

Acts 13:26-52
Jeremiah 15:16

Date _____

WEEK 27 / Friday

Verse of the Day

He showed that their message about his grace was true...

Acts 14:3b

🍎

Thought for the Day

God reaches out his hand and says, "Take My hand. You matter to Me."

Bill Hybels

Acts 14:1-28

Proverbs 3:5-7

Week 27 / Weekend

Date _____

Verse of the Day

When they believed, he made their hearts pure.

Acts 15:9b

Thought for the Day

The emphasis is not on what we do for God; instead, it is on what God has done for us.

Charles Swindoll

Acts 15:1-21
Isaiah 45:22

Date _____

WEEK 28 / Monday

Verse of the Day

So the churches became stronger in the faith and grew larger every day.

Acts 16:5

❦

Thought for the Day

Give (people) at least five minutes, even if you are in a hurry. Stop and pray with them.

Doris Grieg

Acts 15:22-16:10
Proverbs 25:11

WEEK 28 / Tuesday

Date _____

Verse of the Day

About midnight, Paul and Silas were praying and singing songs to God...

Acts 16:25

Thought for the Day

I prayed, I called, I waited... then You accomplished.

Ruth Calkin

Acts 16:11-34
2 Kings 4:8-10

Date _____

WEEK 28 / *Wednesday*

Verse of the Day

"This Jesus I am telling you about is the Christ."

Acts 17:3b

Thought for the Day

Over and above all other things, study the Bible.

Charles Finney

Acts 16:35-17:15

Isaiah 55:10-11

WEEK 28 / Thursday

Date _____

Verse of the Day

We live in him.
We walk in him.
We are in him.

Acts 17:28

Thought for the Day

Jesus Christ is my comfort. It is you who created us all.

Januarius of Cordova

Acts 17:16-18:4

Genesis 2:4-7

Date _____

WEEK 28 / Friday

Verse of the Day

"I am with you, and no one will hurt you..."

Acts 18:10

Thought for the Day

Let us keep our eyes fastened upon Him...

A. B. Simpson

Acts 18:5-28

Psalm 121:5-8

WEEK 28 / Weekend

Date _____

Verse of the Day

Many of the believers began to confess openly and tell all the evil things they had done.

Acts 19:18

❦

Thought for the Day

We need to bring all aspects of our lives under the searching eyes of the Lord.

Jack Hayford

Acts 19:1-22
2 Kings 11:17-18

Date _____

WEEK 29 / Monday

Verse of the Day

He said many things to strengthen the followers in the different places...

Acts 20:2

❦

Thought for the Day

A mighty fortress is our God, a bulwark never failing.

Martin Luther

Acts 19:23-20:6
Psalm 124:2-3, 6-8

WEEK 29 / Tuesday   Date _____

Verse of the Day

I don't care about my own life. The most important thing is that I complete my mission...

Acts 20:24

❧

Thought for the Day

Our Lord was gripped by a master ambition...

J. Oswald Sanders

Acts 20:7-38
1 Kings 18:40

Date _____

WEEK 29 / *Wednesday*

Verse of the Day

"... I am ready to die for the Lord Jesus!"

Acts 21:13b

Thought for the Day

Pray God to send a few men with "grit" in them ...

Charles Spurgeon

Acts 21:1-25

Exodus 32:7, 26-27, 29

WEEK 29 / Thursday

Date _____

Verse of the Day

I persecuted the people who followed the Way of Jesus, and some of them were even killed.

Acts 22:4

Thought for the Day

... don't withhold a drink from someone who is thirsty; it's not just a matter of hospitality, it's a matter of life and death.

Joni Eareckson Tada

Acts 21:26-22:5
Ezekiel 2:3-5

Date _____

WEEK 29 / Friday

Verse of the Day

Later, when I returned to Jerusalem, I was praying in the Temple, and I saw a vision.

Acts 22:17

Thought for the Day

Wait for God. Wait on God. Wait with God.

Anne Ortlund

Acts 22:6-29
Psalm 33:8-12

WEEK 29 / Weekend

Date _____

Verse of the Day

The next night the Lord came and stood by Paul. He said, "Be brave!"

Acts 23:11

❦

Thought for the Day

We are to rely on Him continuously, as our victorious Champion . . .

J. Sydlow Baxter

Acts 22:30–23:22

Psalm 75:1-3

Date _____

WEEK 30 / Monday

Verse of the Day

... I always try to do what I believe is right before God and people.

Acts 24:16

Thought for the Day

If Christ doesn't make any difference in my ethics and values... what difference does He make?

Doug Sherman/ William Hendricks

Acts 23:23-24:16

Jeremiah 22: 15b-16

WEEK 30 / Tuesday

Date _____

Verse of the Day

But Felix became afraid when Paul spoke about living right, self-control . . .

Acts 24:25

Thought for the Day

We have only to realize that God is the Holy Sovereign, and the awe is bound to come back.

John Jones

Acts 24:17-25:12

Genesis 3:7-10

Date _____

WEEK 30 / Wednesday

Verse of the Day

Why do any of you people think it is impossible for God to raise people from the dead?

Acts 26:8

❦

Thought for the Day

We must show nonbelievers what it looks like to be at peace with ourselves . . .

George Barna

Acts 25:13-26:8
2 Samuel 22:21-25

WEEK 30 / Thursday

Date _____

Verse of the Day

The Lord said, "Stand up! I have chosen you to be my servant and my witness..."

Acts 26:16

Thought for the Day

Our lifestyles as Christians should be a testimony to the validity of our message...

Tony Campolo

Acts 26:9-32
Exodus 15:11-14a

Date _____

WEEK 30 / Friday

Verse of the Day

So men, have courage. I trust in God that everything will happen as his angel told me.

Acts 27:25

❦

Thought for the Day

Whatever God promises, God performs. You can count on it.

Woodrow Kroll

Acts 27:1-26
Joshua 1:6-8

Week 30 / Weekend

Date _____

Verse of the Day

None of you will even lose one hair off your heads.

Acts 27:34b

Thought for the Day

If we are in right relationship with God, He will make all that happens to us work out for our good and His glory.

Lucille Sollenberger

Acts 27:27-28:11a
Jonah 1:15-16

Date _____

WEEK 31 / Monday

Verse of the Day

He boldly preached about the kingdom of God and taught about the Lord Jesus Christ . . .

Acts 28:31

❦

Thought for the Day

In the Lord's hands, a few loaves and fishes go a long way.

Rachael Crabb

Acts 28:11b-31

Genesis 24:28, 29a, 30b-32a

WEEK 31 / Tuesday

Date _____

Verse of the Day

As the Scripture says, "But those who are right with God will live by trusting in him."

Romans 1:17b

Thought for the Day

This is my Father's world; He shines in all that's fair.

Maltbie Babcock

Romans 1:1-27
Psalm 19:1-4a

Date _____

WEEK 31 / Wednesday

Verse of the Day

But he will give glory, honor, and peace to everyone who does good...

Romans 2:10

❦

Thought for the Day

God will see that each man sooner or later receives what he deserves—if not here, then hereafter.

J. I. Packer

Romans 1:28-2:16
Proverbs 15:9-11

Week 31 / Thursday

Date _____

Verse of the Day

You have the law; so you think you know everything and have all truth.

Romans 2:20b

❦

Thought for the Day

The fruit of true repentance is a change of mind, heart, and behavior.

Floyd McClung

Romans 2:17-3:18

Jeremiah 7:3, 5-6

Date _____

WEEK 31 / Friday

Verse of the Day

All have sinned and are not good enough for God's glory...

Romans 3:23

❦

Thought for the Day

...He has taken possession of heaven on behalf of His people...

Charles Spurgeon

Romans 3:19-4:12
Psalm 32:10-11

WEEK 31 / Weekend

Date _____

Verse of the Day

He never doubted that God would keep his promise, and he never stopped believing.

Romans 4:20

Thought for the Day

The God who wills only good is a God of love.

Andrew Murray

Romans 4:13-5:11

Isaiah 63:7-9c

Date _____

WEEK 32 / Monday

Verse of the Day

When we were baptized, we were buried with Christ and shared his death.

Romans 6:4

❦

Thought for the Day

If you want to get victory . . . go on to know Christ more intimately.

D. L. Moody

Romans 5:12-6:14
Jeremiah 18:11-12

WEEK 32 / Tuesday

Date _____

Verse of the Day

You are made free from sin, and now you are slaves to goodness.

Romans 6:18

Thought for the Day

Choosing to be chosen means accepting Christ's lordship over our total lives.

Lloyd Ogilvie

Romans 6:15-7:13

Deuteronomy 7:6-8

Date _____

WEEK 32 / Wednesday

Verse of the Day

... I know that nothing good lives in me - I mean nothing good lives in the part of me that is earthly and sinful.

Romans 7:18

❦

Thought for the Day

Choose now whom you will serve, and that choice is going to affect the next generation ...

Edith Schaeffer

Romans 7:14-8:17

Joshua 24:14-15

WEEK 32 / Thursday

Date _____

Verse of the Day

The sufferings we have now are nothing compared to the great glory that will be shown to us.

Romans 8:18

❦

Thought for the Day

His love for me does not in any way depend on my worthiness of it.

Phillip Keller

Romans 8:18-39
Isaiah 59:15b-17, 21

Date _____

WEEK 32 / Friday

Verse of the Day

The potter can make anything he wants to make.

Romans 9:21a

❦

Thought for the Day

You do not understand all . . . because I am God and you are you.

Ruth Senter

Romans 9:1-29

Isaiah 1:9

Week 32 / Weekend

Date _____

Verse of the Day

Christ ended the law so that everyone who believes in him may be right with God.

Romans 10:4

Thought for the Day

The doorway to the kingdom is so low down that one must bend in humility to get through.

Terry Fullam

Romans 9:30-10:21

Isaiah 65:1

Date _____

WEEK 33 / Monday

Verse of the Day

If God did not let the natural branches of that tree stay, then he will not let you stay if you don't believe.

Romans 11:21

❦

Thought for the Day

It is the kindness of God . . . that supplies my salvation.

Phillip Keller

Romans 11:1-21
Ezekiel 18:21-23

Week 33 / Tuesday

Date _____

Verse of the Day

Yes, God's riches are very great, and his wisdom and knowledge have no end!

Romans 11:33

❦

Thought for the Day

Obedience is the soul of knowledge.

George MacDonald

Romans 11:22-12:8

1 Samuel 15:22

Date _____

WEEK 33 / Wednesday

Verse of the Day

Pay everyone, then, what you owe.

Romans 13:7

Thought for the Day

Debt is never the real problem; it is only symptomatic of the real problem...

Ron Blue

Romans 12:9-13:14

Psalm 37:21, 26

WEEK 33 / Thursday

Date _____

Verse of the Day

Anyone who serves Christ by living this way is pleasing God and will be accepted by other people.

Romans 14:18

Thought for the Day

We have forgotten that our purpose is to please God.

Luis Palau

Romans 14:1-15:3

Proverbs 12:14

Date _____

WEEK 33 / Friday

Verse of the Day

The Scriptures give us patience and encouragement so that we can have hope.

Romans 15:4b

❦

Thought for the Day

The more I know Him, the more I experience that deep inner well of joy that is not dependent on circumstances.

Jeanie Miley

Romans 15:4-29
Psalm 33:20-22

WEEK 33 / Weekend

Date _____

Verse of the Day

... be wise in what is good and innocent in what is evil.

Romans 16:19b

Thought for the Day

By modernism, Satan has succeeded in robbing the church of her power in the world.

Herbert Lockyer

Romans 15:30-16:27

Ezekiel 13:3, 7

Date _____

WEEK 34 / Monday

Verse of the Day

Even the foolishness of God is wiser than human wisdom...

1 Corinthians 1:25

❦

Thought for the Day

God is too wise to let man come to know Him by his own wisdom.

James Merritt

1 Corinthians 1:1-25

Isaiah 44:24b-26a

Week 34 / Tuesday

Date _____

Verse of the Day

But God chose the foolish things of the world to shame the wise . . .

1 Corinthians 1:27

Thought for the Day

Since God's wisdom resides in His Word, it is imperative to know what He has revealed.

Rick Yohn

1 Corinthians 1:26-2:16

Job 28:20-28

Date _____

Week 34 / Wednesday

Verse of the Day

We are God's workers, working together...

1 Corinthians 3:9

❦

Thought for the Day

A life built on Jesus and His teachings will stand...

James Boice

1 Corinthians 3:1-4:5

Psalm 118:22

Week 34 / Thursday

Date _____

Verse of the Day

We are fools for Christ's sake . . .

1 Corinthians 4:10

Thought for the Day

No Christian can entertain sin and get away with it.

George Sweeting/ Donald Sweeting

1 Corinthians 4:6-5:8

Deuteronomy 17:2, 4b-5, 12

Date _____

WEEK 34 / Friday

Verse of the Day

I am allowed to do all things, but all things are not good for me to do.

1 Corinthians 6:12a

Thought for the Day

Our thoughts are the fabric with which we weave our character and destiny.

Randy Alcorn

1 Corinthians 5:9-6:20

Proverbs 6:27-29

WEEK 34 / Weekend

Date _____

Verse of the Day

Brothers and sisters, each of you should stay as you were when you were called, and stay there with God.

1 Corinthians 7:24

Thought for the Day

A marriage well-oiled by grace is durable and protected against the wear and tear of friction.

Charles Swindoll

1 Corinthians 7:1-24

Malachi 2:15-16b

Date _____

WEEK 35 / Monday

Verse of the Day

Knowledge puffs you up with pride, but love builds up.

1 Corinthians 8:1b

❦

Thought for the Day

No one should enter marriage without realizing the time and energy required to make it work.

Richard Foster

1 Corinthians 7:25-8:8

Jeremiah 1:4-5; 9-10, 16:1-2

WEEK 35 / Tuesday

Date _____

Verse of the Day

But be careful that your freedom does not cause those who are weak in faith to fall into sin.

1 Corinthians 8:9

❦

Thought for the Day

The disciple must choose his priorities very carefully . . .

J. Oswald Sanders

1 Corinthians 8:9-9:18

Amos 2:11-14

Date _____

WEEK 35 / *Wednesday*

Verse of the Day

You know that in a race all the runners run, but only one gets the prize.

1 Corinthians 9:24

❧

Thought for the Day

Saying no when you want to say yes builds character.

Jill Briscoe

1 Corinthians 9:19-10:22

John 2:3-10

Week 35 / Thursday

Date _____

Verse of the Day

Do not look out only for yourselves. Look out for the good of others also.

1 Corinthians 10:24

Thought for the Day

Those who are really committed to excellence give Him top priority.

Charles Swindoll

1 Corinthians 10:23-11:22

1 Samuel 2:12, 30-31

Date _____

Week 35 / Friday

Verse of the Day

And there are different ways that God works through people, but only one God.

1 Corinthians 12:6a

❦

Thought for the Day

If you want to be used by our Lord, it will pay us to ferret out what our ability is, then get busy putting it to use.

Jeanette Lockerbie

1 Corinthians 11:23-12:13

Deuteronomy 34:9

Week 35 / Weekend

Date _____

Verse of the Day

But even with all these things, if I do not have love, I am nothing.

1 Corinthians 13:2b

Thought for the Day

We are to love with the kind of love our Master has shown to us.
William Fletcher

1 Corinthians 12:14-13:13

Ruth 2:14-16

Date _____

WEEK 36 / Monday

Verse of the Day

You should seek after love, and you should truly want to have the spiritual gifts.

1 Corinthians 14:1

❦

Thought for the Day

God has given each of us a task to do, and supernatural gifts to equip us for it.

Billy Graham

1 Corinthians 14:1-25

2 Kings 23:15-16

WEEK 36 / Tuesday

Date _____

Verse of the Day

God is not a God of confusion but a God of peace.

1 Corinthians 14:33

❦

Thought for the Day

God, very God, in Christ takes my sins and gives me His righteousness.

Phillip Keller

1 Corinthians 14:26-15:11

Psalm 47:5-8

Date _____

WEEK 36 / Wednesday

Verse of the Day

In Adam all of us die. In the same way, in Christ all of us will be made alive again.

1 Corinthians 15:22

Thought for the Day

In a little while we shall be as Jesus now is.

Charles Spurgeon

1 Corinthians 15:12-44a

Daniel 12:2-3

WEEK 36 / Thursday

Date _____

Verse of the Day

Be alert. Continue strong in the faith. Have courage, and be strong.

1 Corinthians 16:13

❦

Thought for the Day

. . . Christ-like conduct is proof positive that I am indeed God's person.

Phillip Keller

1 Corinthians 15:44b-16:24

Psalm 35:1, 7

Date _____

WEEK 36 / Friday

Verse of the Day

God is the Father who is full of mercy and all comfort.

2 Corinthians 1:3b

❦

Thought for the Day

Everything becomes a "chariot of salvation" when God rides upon it.

Hannah Whitall Smith

2 Corinthians 1:1-17

Psalm 56:1-4

WEEK 36 / Weekend

Date _____

Verse of the Day

God uses us to spread his knowledge everywhere like a sweet-smelling perfume.

2 Corinthians 2:14b

Thought for the Day

We need to live in the light of His countenance daily.

Andrew Murray

2 Corinthians 1:18-3:3

Genesis 50:16-17, 19-21

Date _____

WEEK 37 / Monday

Verse of the Day

We will all show the Lord's glory, and we are being changed to be like him.

2 Corinthians 3:18

❦

Thought for the Day

Holiness, love, compassion, justice, truth, or mercy - that's God's glory.

Joni Eareckson Tada

2 Corinthians 3:4-4:15
Job 24:13, 23-24

Week 37 / Tuesday

Date _____

Verse of the Day

We set our eyes not on what we see, but on what we cannot see.

2 Corinthians 4:18

Thought for the Day

As for our souls, we cannot guess to what an elevation it shall be raised in Christ Jesus.

Charles Spurgeon

2 Corinthians 4:16-6:2

Psalm 24:3-6

Date _____

WEEK 37 / Wednesday

Verse of the Day

We should try to become holy in the way we live, because we respect God.

2 Corinthians 7:1b

Thought for the Day

Someone has said, "a belief is what you hold; a conviction is what holds you."

Jerry Bridges

2 Corinthians 6:3-7:7

Proverbs 4:14-15

WEEK 37 / Thursday

Date _____

Verse of the Day

You know that Christ was rich, but for you he became poor . . .

2 Corinthians 8:9

Thought for the Day

Repentance is simply and precisely a change of mind.

Charles Finney

2 Corinthians 7:8-8:15
Ezra 10:1-3b

Date _____

Week 37 / Friday

Verse of the Day

God loves the person who gives happily.

2 Corinthians 9:7b

Thought for the Day

Sharing with others is the way to real joy.

Ronald Sider

2 Corinthians 8:16-9:15

Proverbs 28:27

Week 37 / Weekend

Date _____

Verse of the Day

But, "If someone wants to brag, he should brag only about the Lord."

2 Corinthians 10:17

❧

Thought for the Day

Might lies with the Father who is almighty.

Charles Spurgeon

2 Corinthians 10:1-11:4

2 Chronicles 20:20-22

Date _____

Week 38 / Monday

Verse of the Day

If I must brag, I will brag about the things that show I am weak.

2 Corinthians 11:30

Thought for the Day

We grow in our understanding through difficulties, as God opens to us that which we could not have understood with any other background.

Edith Schaeffer

2 Corinthians 11:5-33

Exodus 1:22

WEEK 38 / Tuesday

Date _____

Verse of the Day

"My grace is enough for you."

2 Corinthians 12:9

Thought for the Day

Relying on the power of Christ, I become capable of whatever the Lord requires of me.

Charles Stanley

2 Corinthians 12:1-13:4

1 Samuel 30:6b, 8

Date _____

WEEK 38 / Wednesday

Verse of the Day

Agree with each other, and live in peace.

2 Corinthians 13:11b

❦

Thought for the Day

God's way for us is always better than our own.

J. R. Miller

2 Corinthians 13:5 - Galatians 1:21
1 Samuel 9:17

WEEK 38 / Thursday

Date _____

Verse of the Day

I do not live anymore, it is Christ who lives in me.

Galatians 2:20

❦

Thought for the Day

It is the self-sacrifice of Christ we are to imitate as we relate to the poor and oppressed . . .

Ronald Sider

Galatians 1:22-2:21

Proverbs 21:13

Date _____

WEEK 38 / Friday

Verse of the Day

Christ took away the curse the law put on us.

Galatians 3:13a

❦

Thought for the Day

Count your many blessings and see what God hath done.

Johnson Oatman, Jr.

Galatians 3:1-20
Genesis 22:15-17a

WEEK 38 / Weekend

Date _____

Verse of the Day

... God sent the Spirit of his Son into your hearts, and the Spirit cries out, "Father."

Galatians 4:6

Thought for the Day

He will constantly be showing us more and more of his love ...

J.I. Packer

Galatians 3:21-4:20

Isaiah 64:8-9

Date _____

WEEK 39 / Monday

Verse of the Day

Serve each other with love.

Galatians 5:13b

❦

Thought for the Day

Christian liberty is the freedom to love and to serve.

Lucille Sollenberger

Galatians 4:21-5:15

Genesis 21:8-12

WEEK 39 / Tuesday

Date _____

Verse of the Day

If anyone thinks he is important when he really is not, he is only fooling himself.

Galatians 6:3

Thought for the Day

Idols are anything that steals our hearts away from the Lord...

David Reid

Galatians 5:16-6:18

Ecclesiastes 2:26

Date _____

WEEK 39 / Wednesday

Verse of the Day

In Christ, God has given us every spiritual blessing in the heavenly world.

Ephesians 1:3

❧

Thought for the Day

We cannot heal, but God can heal through us.

Margaret Magdalen

Ephesians 1:1-2:3
Job 42:8b-9

Week 39 / Thursday

Date _____

Verse of the Day

But God's mercy is great, and he loved us very much.

Ephesians 2:4

Thought for the Day

Nothing else will so move our stony spirits to extend mercy.

Phillip Keller

Ephesians 2:4-3:6
Micah 7:18-19a

Date _____

WEEK 39 / Friday

Verse of the Day

In Christ we can come before God with freedom and without fear.

Ephesians 3:12

❦

Thought for the Day

Oh let this love fill our hearts with adoring gratitude . . .

Charles Spurgeon

Ephesians 3:7-4:16
Psalm 136:1, 4

Week 39 / Weekend

Date _____

Verse of the Day

Be kind and loving to each other, and forgive each other just as God forgave you in Christ.

Ephesians 4:32

Thought for the Day

How we need to hear the voice of the New Testament as it calls us to a life of responsible stewardship . . .

Art Beals

Ephesians 4:17-5:14

Proverbs 30:15-16

Date _____

WEEK 40 / Monday

Verse of the Day

Husbands, love your wives as Christ loved the church and gave himself for it.

Ephesians 5:25

❦

Thought for the Day

Loving headship delights to delegate without demanding.

H. Norman Wright

Ephesians 5:15-6:4

Song of Solomon 2:16-17

WEEK 40 / Tuesday

Date _____

Verse of the Day

Finally, be strong in the Lord and in his great power.

Ephesians 6:10

Thought for the Day

We are to acknowledge our weakness and invite His power.

R. Kent Hughes

Ephesians 6:5-24

Job 1:6-10

Date _____

WEEK 40 / Wednesday

Verse of the Day

Instead, be humble and give more honor to others than to yourselves.

Philippians 2:3b

❦

Thought for the Day

The disposition of the humble person is to wholly submit himself to God.

Jonathan Edwards

Philippians 1:1-2:4

Micah 6:8

Week 40 / Thursday

Date _____

Verse of the Day

Your faith makes you offer your lives as a sacrifice in serving God.

Philippians 2:17

❦

Thought for the Day

How is it possible to give thanks and complain at the same time?

Madalene Harris

Philippians 2:5-30

Proverbs 20:3

Date _____

WEEK 40 / Friday

Verse of the Day

I keep trying to reach the goal and get the prize for which God called me through Christ . . .

Philippians 3:14

❦

Thought for the Day

. . . the disciple must run his race with eyes steadfastly fixed on his encouraging Lord.

J. Oswald Sanders

Philippians 3:1-21

Psalm 42:1-2

Week 40 / Weekend

Date _____

Verse of the Day

Do not worry about anything, but pray and ask God for everything you need . . .

Philippians 4:6

Thought for the Day

Whatever your needs are right now, trust God to meet them and look for His supply.

John Witmer

Philippians 4:1-23
Psalm 55:22

Date _____

WEEK 41 / *Monday*

Verse of the Day

God will strengthen you with his own great power so that you will not give up when troubles come.

Colossians 1:11

❦

Thought for the Day

... as Christians, we can find stability and hope in Jesus who is the sovereign Lord of history.

J. I. Packer

Colossians 1:1-23

Isaiah 41:2a-b, 4

Week 41 / Tuesday

Date _____

Verse of the Day

Keep your roots deep in him and have your lives built on him.

Colossians 2:7

❦

Thought for the Day

... when the worst storm blows ... it will be said of your faith, "It could not shake it."

Charles Spurgeon

Colossians 1:24-2:15

Psalm 40:1-4

Date _____

WEEK 41 / Wednesday

Verse of the Day

Let the teaching of Christ live in you richly.

Colossians 3:16

❦

Thought for the Day

God's Word must be so fixed in our minds that it becomes the dominant influence…

Jerry Bridges

Colossians 2:16-3:17

Leviticus 20:7-8, 26

WEEK 41 / Thursday

Date _____

Verse of the Day

Children, obey your parents in all things...

Colossians 3:20

Thought for the Day

Obedience is its own reward.

Jeanette Lockerbie

Colossians 3:18-4:18

Proverbs 6:20-22

Date _____

WEEK 41 / Friday

Verse of the Day

He is Jesus, who saves us from God's angry judgment that is sure to come.

1 Thessalonians 1:10b

❦

Thought for the Day

Our Savior is the harbor of weather-beaten sails.

Charles Spurgeon

1 Thessalonians 1:1-2:16

Deuteronomy 7:7-8a

Week 41 / Weekend

Date _____

Verse of the Day

Our life is really full if you stand strong in the Lord.

1 Thessalonians 3:8

❧

Thought for the Day

The Holy Spirit does not save us without giving us the desire to live a holy life.

Floyd McClung

1 Thessalonians 2:17-4:12

Leviticus 22:31-33

Date _____

WEEK 42 / Monday

Verse of the Day

... the day the Lord comes again will be a surprise, like a thief that comes in the night.

1 Thessalonians 5:2

❦

Thought for the Day

Jesus Christ has fulfilled every promise He ever made.

Billy Graham

1 Thessalonians 4:13-5:28

Job 19:25-27

WEEK 42 / Tuesday

Date _____

Verse of the Day

He wants you to be counted worthy of his kingdom for which you are suffering.

2 Thessalonians 1:5

Thought for the Day

What an exhibition of His purpose to sustain the interests of holiness . . . in all His vast dominions!

Charles Finney

2 Thessalonians 1:1-2:12
Isaiah 1:27-28

Date _____

WEEK 42 / Wednesday

Verse of the Day

But the Lord is faithful and will give you strength and will protect you from the Evil One.

2 Thessalonians 3:3

Thought for the Day

... your life has been appointed by God's wise providence.

F. B. Meyer

2 Thessalonians 2:13-3:18
Proverbs 31:10-16

WEEK 42 / Thursday Date _____

Verse of the Day

Continue to have faith and do what you know is right.

1 Timothy 1:19

🍃

Thought for the Day

... we should be imitators of God and show mercy to those God brings our way.

Elliot Johnson/ Al Scheirbaum

1 Timothy 1:1-20

Isaiah 55:7

Date _____

WEEK 42 / Friday

Verse of the Day

There is one God and one way human beings can reach God.

1 Timothy 2:5

❦

Thought for the Day

Men have always stumbled over the simplicity of salvation.

John F. MacArthur, Jr.

1 Timothy 2:1-3:13

Deuteronomy 4:34-38

WEEK 42 / *Weekend*

Date _____

Verse of the Day

... be an example to the believers with your words, your actions, your love, your faith, and your pure life.

1 Timothy 4:12b

Thought for the Day

Jesus had compassion, but there was a toughness in this love.

Rebecca Pippert

1 Timothy 3:14-4:16

2 Kings 23:3, 24-25

Date _____

WEEK 43 / Monday

Verse of the Day

Whoever does not care for his own family . . . is worse than someone who does not believe in God.

1 Timothy 5:8

❦

Thought for the Day

. . . often, Christians who know precisely what is wrong will not love sufficiently to tackle the problem.

Howard and Jeanne Hendricks

1 Timothy 5:1-25
2 Samuel 12:7, 9, 13-14

Week 43 / Tuesday

Date _____

Verse of the Day

Serving God does make us very rich, if we are satisfied with what we have.

1 Timothy 6:6

Thought for the Day

God often allows people to accumulate property so they may have an opportunity to extend the cause of truth . . .

Charles Finney

1 Timothy 6:1-21

Ecclesiastes 5:19-20

Date _____   WEEK 43 / Wednesday

Verse of the Day

So do not be ashamed to tell people about our Lord Jesus . . .

2 Timothy 1:8

Thought for the Day

It takes a disciple-maker to make disciples.

Walter Henrichsen

2 Timothy 1:1-2:13

Deuteronomy 4:9-10

WEEK 43 / Thursday

Date _____

Verse of the Day

All who make themselves clean from evil will be used for special purposes.

2 Timothy 2:21

❦

Thought for the Day

If we want to train ourselves to be godly, it must be holiness in every area of our lives.

Jerry Bridges

2 Timothy 2:14-3:11

Psalm 101:1-5

Date _____

WEEK 43 / Friday

Verse of the Day

All scripture is given by God and is useful for teaching, for showing people what is wrong... for correcting faults, and for teaching how to live right.

2 Timothy 3:16

🍎

Thought for the Day

God's Word, like a deep, deep mine, stands ready to yield its treasures.

Charles Swindoll

2 Timothy 3:12-4:22

Nehemiah 8:8, 14-15

WEEK 43 / Weekend

Date _____

Verse of the Day

To the pure all things are pure...

Titus 1:15

Thought for the Day

Be blameless. This quality we should strive for whether or not we are in positions of church leadership.

Gene Getz

Titus 1:1-2:8
Malachi 2:7-9

Date _____

WEEK 44 / *Monday*

Verse of the Day

He saved us through the washing that made us new people through the Holy Spirit.

Titus 3:5b

❦

Thought for the Day

God is aware of the whisper, "I love you, God."

Edith Schaeffer

Titus 2:9-3:15

Daniel 6:21-22, 25-27

WEEK 44 / Tuesday   Date _____

Verse of the Day

I have great joy and comfort, my brother, because the love you have shown to God's people has refreshed them.

Philemon 1:7

Thought for the Day

We live from a posture of knowing that we are loved.

Bill Gillham

Philemon 1-25

Genesis 41:39-40, 42-43

Date _____

WEEK 44 / Wednesday

Verse of the Day

The Son reflects the glory of God and shows exactly what God is like.

Hebrews 1:3

❦

Thought for the Day

Rejoicing and salvation belong together.

William Stoddard

Hebrews 1:1-2:4
Psalm 86:11-13

Week 44 / Thursday

Date _____

Verse of the Day

God is the One who made all things, and all things are for his glory.

Hebrews 2:10

❦

Thought for the Day

. . . becoming more holy is God's work in us . . .

Patrick Morley

Hebrews 2:5-3:6

Ezekiel 37:22, 23b-28

Date _____

WEEK 44 / Friday

Verse of the Day

We who have believed are able to enter and have God's rest.

Hebrews 4:3

❦

Thought for the Day

We must put into practical obedience the knowledge that we have.

Rebecca Pippert

Hebrews 3:7—4:13

Numbers 14:8-9, 20-23

Week 44 / Weekend

Date _____

Verse of the Day

Even though Jesus was the Son of God, he learned obedience by what he suffered.

Hebrews 5:8

Thought for the Day

We have access to His grace, but even more, we have access to Him.

R. C. Sproul

Hebrews 4:14-6:8

Exodus 28:1-3

Date _____

WEEK 45 / Monday

Verse of the Day

God is fair, he will not forget the work you did and the love you showed...

Hebrews 6:10

❦

Thought for the Day

God had already provided the answer to your every need before the world was ever formed.

Richard Lee

Hebrews 6:9-7:10

Joshua 23:5-6, 14-16

Week 45 / Tuesday

Date _____

Verse of the Day

... he is able always to save those who come to God through him because he always lives, asking God to help them.

Hebrews 7:25

❦

Thought for the Day

... we need the high priestly mediation of our dear heavenly Advocate.

J. Sydlow Baxter

Hebrews 7:11-8:6
Jeremiah 31:33

Date _____

WEEK 45 / Wednesday

Verse of the Day

His sacrifice was his own blood, and by it he set us free from sin forever.

Hebrews 9:12b

❣

Thought for the Day

At the center of forgiveness is always the cross of Christ.

David McKenna

Hebrews 8:7-9:12
Isaiah 53:10-11

WEEK 45 / Thursday

Date _____

Verse of the Day

His blood will make our consciences pure from useless acts so we may serve the living God.

Hebrews 9:14b

Thought for the Day

When we sin, our only option is repentance.

R. C. Sproul

Hebrews 9:13-10:10

Leviticus 16:15, 17b, 34

Date _____

WEEK 45 / Friday

Verse of the Day

...let us come near to God with a sincere heart and a sure faith...

Hebrews 10:22

❦

Thought for the Day

If we refuse to turn to God's mercy...we condemn ourselves...

Richard Halverson

Hebrews 10:11-39

Amos 5:14

WEEK 45 / Weekend

Date _____

Verse of the Day

Faith means being sure of the things we hope for...

Hebrews 11:1

Thought for the Day

Whenever He found even the tiniest fragment of faith... He was delighted.

Phillip Keller

Hebrews 11:1-22

Genesis 15:5-6

Date _____

WEEK 46 / Monday

Verse of the Day

Let us look only to Jesus, the One who began our faith and who makes it perfect.

Hebrews 12:2

🍃

Thought for the Day

Can I expect . . . the shaping of my character . . . to be any less time-consuming?

Phillip Keller

Hebrews 11:23-12:6

Job 5:17-18

WEEK 46 / Tuesday

Date _____

Verse of the Day

But God disciplines us to help us, so we can become holy as he is.

Hebrews 12:10b

Thought for the Day

. . . God's sovereignty will never clash with His paternity.

J. Oswald Sanders

Hebrews 12:7-29

2 Samuel 24:10, 15a, 17-19, 25b

Date _____

WEEK 46 / Wednesday

Verse of the Day

Keep your lives free from the love of money.

Hebrews 13:5

❦

Thought for the Day

The Christian life is the life of obedience and submission which result in joy and victory.

Bill Bright

Hebrews 13:1-25

Deuteronomy 10:12b-13, 16, 18-21

WEEK 46 / Thursday

Date _____

Verse of the Day

But when you ask God, you must believe and not doubt.

James 1:6

Thought for the Day

Someone has said, "Doubt is a non-conductor of grace."

Millie Stamm

James 1:1-27
1 Kings 3:10-13

Date _____

WEEK 46 / Friday

Verse of the Day

... faith that is alone, that does nothing, is dead.

James 2:17

❦

Thought for the Day

... we must extend genuine mercy to our contemporaries.

Phillip Keller

James 2:1-26

Obadiah 13-14

WEEK 46 / Weekend

Date _____

Verse of the Day

So give yourselves completely to God. Stand against the devil, and the devil will run from you.

James 4:7

Thought for the Day

We need to constantly fill the heart with good things from God's Word...

Vicki Lake

James 3:1-4:10
Proverbs 18:20-21

Date _____

WEEK 47 / Monday

Verse of the Day

Confess your sins to each other and pray for each other so God can heal you.

James 5:16

🍂

Thought for the Day

Through prayer we can open a window to God's love . . .

Warren Myers

James 4:11-5:20

Esther 4:15-16

Week 47 / Tuesday

Date _____

Verse of the Day

So you are filled with a joy that can not be explained, a joy full of glory.

1 Peter 1:8b

❦

Thought for the Day

I think sorrows usually bring us closer to God than joys do.

Henry Beecher

1 Peter 1:1-21
Zechariah 13:9

Date _____

WEEK 47/ Wednesday

Verse of the Day

So love each other deeply with all your heart.

1 Peter 1:22b

❦

Thought for the Day

Exalted piety is honorable to God.

Charles Finney

1 Peter 1:22-2:17

Daniel 3:28-29

Week 47 / Thursday

Date _____

Verse of the Day

. . . your beauty should come from within you . . .

1 Peter 3:4

❧

Thought for the Day

The peace of God produces healing.

Phillip Keller

1 Peter 2:18-3:12

Genesis 26:26-31

Date _____

WEEK 47 / Friday

Verse of the Day

Always be ready to answer everyone who asks you to explain about the hope you have . . .

1 Peter 3:15b

🍂

Thought for the Day

And the great thing about our hope is that it is based on fact.

YFC Editors

1 Peter 3:13-4:11
Psalm 71:12-16

WEEK 47 / Weekend

Date _____

Verse of the Day

Give all your worries to him, because he cares about you.

1 Peter 5:7

Thought for the Day

My faith increased, as I learned to trust God for my every need.

Barbara Hyatt

1 Peter 4:12-5:14
1 Kings 17:2-4, 6-9

Date _____

WEEK 48 / Monday

Verse of the Day

No prophecy ever came from what a person wanted to say, but people led by the Holy Spirit . . . .

2 Peter 1:21

❦

Thought for the Day

We can not rely on pastors or Christian leaders to keep our faith propped up.

Floyd McClung

2 Peter 1:1-21

Proverbs 1:1, 3, 7

WEEK 48 / Tuesday

Date _____

Verse of the Day

These false teachers left the right road and lost their way . . .

2 Peter 2:15

❦

Thought for the Day

Deception is on the rise within the Christian church and we ignore it to our peril.

Billy Graham

2 Peter 2:1-22

Isaiah 56:11

Date _____

WEEK 48 / Wednesday

Verse of the Day

But grow in the grace and knowledge of our Lord and Savior Jesus Christ.

2 Peter 3:18a

Thought for the Day

Rejoice and actually leap for joy!

H. Norman Wright

2 Peter 3:1-18

Psalm 22:3-8

WEEK 48 / Thursday

Date _____

Verse of the Day

... live in the light, as God is in the light ...

1 John 1:7a

❦

Thought for the Day

Don't attempt to show off how bright and sparkling you are, just shine!

Charles Swindoll

1 John 1:1-2:14

Job 38:15a

Date _____

WEEK 48 / Friday

Verse of the Day

Do not love the world or the things in the world.

1 John 2:15

❦

Thought for the Day

... the true purpose of our existence in this world is to love God ...

Malcolm Muggeridge

1 John 2:15-3:10

Ecclesiastes 2:10-11

Week 48 / Weekend

Date _____

Verse of the Day

This is how we know what real love is: Jesus gave his life for us.

1 John 3:16

Thought for the Day

Being a Christian involves a commitment to treat others as He would treat them.

Tony Campolo

1 John 3:11-4:12
2 Samuel 9:3, 5-7

Date _____

WEEK 49 / Monday

Verse of the Day

God is love. Those who live in love live in God …

1 John 4:16b

♥

Thought for the Day

God says, I want to know you. You count with me.

Ruth Senter

1 John 4:13-5:21

Psalm 66:19-20

WEEK 49 / Tuesday

Date _____

Verse of the Day

Nothing gives me greater joy than to hear that my children are following the way of truth.

3 John 4

❦

Thought for the Day

All of us need encouragement - someone to believe in us.

Charles Swindoll

2 John 1 - 3 John 15

Deuteronomy 31:7-8

Date _____

WEEK 49 / Wednesday

Verse of the Day

Fight hard for the faith . . .

Jude 3

Thought for the Day

He must sustain His throne and save His loyal subjects.

Charles Finney

Jude 1-13

Isaiah 13:6-11

WEEK 49 / Thursday

Date _____

Verse of the Day

God is strong and can help you not to fall.

Jude 24

Thought for the Day

Rebellion, be it active or passive, calls for justice.

Ruth Senter

Jude 14-25
Jeremiah 9:23-24

Date _____

WEEK 49 / Friday

Verse of the Day

"Do not be afraid. I am the First and the Last."

Revelation 1:17b

Thought for the Day

I am your health, your energy: I bring you to a "finish."

Marie Chapman

Revelation 1:1-20

Isaiah 48:12-13

Week 49 / Weekend

Date _____

Verse of the Day

So remember where you were before you fell.

Revelation 2:5

🍂

Thought for the Day

Each of us forgets too soon. We all have the inherent tendency to drift from God.

George Sweeting/ Donald Sweeting

Revelation 2:1-17

Jeremiah 3:12

Date _____

Week 50 / Monday

Verse of the Day

Only continue in your loyalty until I come.

Revelation 2:25

❦

Thought for the Day

We must ask God for the determination to overcome sin.

David Mains

Revelation 2:18-3:6

Deuteronomy 10:12

WEEK 50 / Tuesday

Date _____

Verse of the Day

I am coming soon. Continue strong in your faith so no one will take away your crown.

Revelation 3:11

❦

Thought for the Day

It seemed the Lord put His hand on my shoulder and said, "But you're not home yet."

Donald McCullough

Revelation 3:7-4:5

Daniel 12:1-3

Date _____

WEEK 50 / Wednesday

Verse of the Day

"The Lamb who was killed is worthy..."

Revelation 5:12a

❣

Thought for the Day

Behind the universe there is a Power worthy of our praise and of our trust.

Billy Graham

Revelation 4:6-6:2

Isaiah 6:1-5

WEEK 50 / Thursday

Date _____

Verse of the Day

These souls shouted in a loud voice, "Holy and true Lord, how long until you judge the people of the earth and punish them for killing us?"

Revelation 6:10

❦

Thought for the Day

... there will be no general or mass turning to God in repentance, but only a turning from God's face.

Charles Ryrie

Revelation 6:3-7:8
Nahum 1:2a, 5-6a

Date _____

Week 50 / Friday

Verse of the Day

... "Salvation belongs to our God, who sits on the throne, and to the Lamb."

Revelation 7:10

🍎

Thought for the Day

He is the Lamb in that He is meek and lowly in heart, gentle and unresisting, and all the time surrendering His own will to the Father's ...

Roy and Revel Hession

Revelation 7:9-8:13

Isaiah 61:10

WEEK 50/ Weekend

Date _____

Verse of the Day

These people did not change their hearts and turn away from murder or evil magic...

Revelation 9:21

❦

Thought for the Day

...the flood gates shall soon be opened: the thunderbolts of God are yet in His storehouse.

Charles Spurgeon

Revelation 9:1-10:4

Joel 2:1b, 10-12

Date _____

WEEK 51 / Monday

Verse of the Day

"Take the scroll and eat it. It will be sour in your stomach, but in your mouth it will be sweet as honey."

Revelation 10:9b

🍎

Thought for the Day

When the enemies of the truth have deemed themselves triumphant, there has been a rekindling of gospel testimony.

F. B. Meyer

Revelation 10:5-11:14

1 Kings 17:1; 18:1-2

WEEK 51 / Tuesday

Date _____

Verse of the Day

"The power to rule the world now belongs to our Lord and his Christ..."

Revelation 11:15b

❦

Thought for the Day

...the church can always defeat the enemy by being faithful to Jesus Christ.

Warren Wiersbe

Revelation 11:15-12:12

Daniel 7:21-22

Date _____

WEEK 51/ Wednesday

Verse of the Day

Let the one who has understanding find the meaning of the number . . .

Revelation 13:18b

❦

Thought for the Day

We must be entrenched in the strength of the Lord.

Evan Hopkins

Revelation 12:13-13:18

Daniel 11:32-35

WEEK 51 / Thursday

Date _____

Verse of the Day

So worship God who made the heavens and the earth . . .

Revelation 14:7b

❦

Thought for the Day

The sinner's peace is that terribly prophetic calm . . .

Charles Spurgeon

Revelation 14:1-20

Jeremiah 25:15-17, 26b

Date _____

Week 51 / Friday

Verse of the Day

Everything the Lord does is right and true...

Revelation 15:3b

🌱

Thought for the Day

As victor, He wears the illustrious crown...

Charles Spurgeon

Revelation 15:1-16:11

Deuteronomy 32:19-20, 23-24

Week 51 / Weekend

Date _____

Verse of the Day

"Listen! I will come as a thief comes."

Revelation 16:15

❦

Thought for the Day

God's wrath is the evidence of His holy love for all that is right . . .

Warren Wiersbe

Revelation 16:12-17:8

Ezekiel 38:18-23

Date _____

WEEK 52 / Monday

Verse of the Day

They shall make war against the Lamb, but the Lamb will defeat them ...

Revelation 17:14

❦

Thought for the Day

Though sin no longer has dominion over us, it wages its guerrilla warfare against us.

Jerry Bridges

Revelation 17:9-18:10

Genesis 19:15

Week 52 / Tuesday

Date _____

Verse of the Day

"Be happy because of this, heaven!"

Revelation 18:20

❦

Thought for the Day

God's vengeance will be revealed...

David Hocking

Revelation 18:11-24

Jeremiah 51:25-26, 36a

Date _____

WEEK 52 / Wednesday

Verse of the Day

Salvation, glory and power belong to our God.

Revelation 19:1b

Thought for the Day

In heaven . . . a new celebration, sponsored by God, has gotten under way.

Tony Campolo

Revelation 19:1-16

Exodus 15:11-13, 17-18

Week 52 / Thursday

Date _____

Verse of the Day

I saw an angel coming down from heaven.

Revelation 20:1

🍃

Thought for the Day

For thousands of years, Satan has seduced nations into thinking that they can build a world of peace... without Christ.

David Jeremiah

Revelation 19:17-20:15

Ezekiel 39:1, 4-8

Date _____

Week 52 / Friday

Verse of the Day

He will wipe away every tear from their eyes . . .

Revelation 21:4

❦

Thought for the Day

Jesus is preparing the new Jerusalem for us now.

David Jeremiah

Revelation 21:1-27

Zachariah 2:10-13

Week 52/ Weekend

Date _____

Verse of the Day

"... I am the bright morning star."

Revelation 22:16b

❦

Thought for the Day

Come celebrate the living water that flows for you in an eternal spring.

Ruth Senter

Revelation 22:1-21

Psalm 46:4-5a

Scripture Reading Checklist

	New Testament	*Old Testament*

Week 1
- ☐ Monday — Matthew 1:1-25 — Isaiah 7:13-14
- ☐ Tuesday — Matthew 2:1-23 — Micah 5:2-5a
- ☐ Wednesday — Matthew 3:1-4:11 — Psalm 34:11-14
- ☐ Thursday — Matthew 4:12-5:12 — Genesis 12:1, 2, 4
- ☐ Friday — Matthew 5:13-37 — Psalm 97:10-11
- ☐ Weekend — Matthew 5:38-6:15 — Psalm 25:4-7

Week 2
- ☐ Monday — Matthew 6:16–7:6 — Nehemiah 9:1-3
- ☐ Tuesday — Matthew 7:7–8:4 — Psalm 1:1-3
- ☐ Wednesday — Matthew 8:5–27 — Psalm 104:1-4, 31-33
- ☐ Thursday — Matthew 8:28–9:17 — Psalm 103:8-13
- ☐ Friday — Matthew 9:8–10:10 — Ezekiel 34:15-16
- ☐ Weekend — Matthew 10:11–40 — Jeremiah 20:8c-9

Week 3
- ☐ Monday — Matthew 10:41-11:24 — Proverbs 1:22a, 24-26a, 28-31
- ☐ Tuesday — Matthew 11:25-12:21 — Psalm 51:17
- ☐ Wednesday — Matthew 12:22-45 — Proverbs 10:20-21
- ☐ Thursday — Matthew 12:46-13:17 — Zechariah 7:11-12
- ☐ Friday — Matthew 13:18-43 — Deuteronomy 11:18-21
- ☐ Weekend — Matthew 13:44-14:12 — Psalm 145:10-13a

Week 4
- ☐ Monday — Matthew 14:13-36 — Psalm 116:5-9
- ☐ Tuesday — Matthew 15:1-31 — Proverbs 26:24-26
- ☐ Wednesday — Matthew 15:32-16:20 — Isaiah 55:1-2
- ☐ Thursday — Matthew 16:21-17:13 — Isaiah 53:6-10
- ☐ Friday — Matthew 17:14-18:9 — 2 Chronicles 33:12-13
- ☐ Weekend — Matthew 18:10-35 — Ezekiel 18:21-23

Week 5
- ☐ Monday — Matthew 19:1-26 — Malachi 2:13-16
- ☐ Tuesday — Matthew 19:27-20:19 — 1 Samuel 2:2, 6-8b
- ☐ Wednesday — Matthew 20:20-21:11 — Psalm 95:1-3
- ☐ Thursday — Matthew 21:12-32 — Psalm 26:8
- ☐ Friday — Matthew 21:33-22:14 — Isaiah 56:3-5
- ☐ Weekend — Mattthew 22:15-40 — Deuteronomy 6:4-9

Week 6
- ☐ Monday — Matthew 22:41-23:22 — Jeremiah 5:30-31
- ☐ Tuesday — Matthew 23:23-24:8 — Psalm 94:20-23
- ☐ Wednesday — Matthew 24:9-35 — Isaiah 13:9-10
- ☐ Thursday — Matthew 24:36-25:13 — Malachi 3:1, 2, 5, 16-18
- ☐ Friday — Matthew 25:14-40 — Psalm 41:1-3
- ☐ Weekend — Matthew 25:41-26:19 — Judges 13:15-23

	New Testament	*Old Testament*

Week 7
- ☐ Monday — Matthew 26:20-46 — Ezekiel 34:11-12,16a
- ☐ Tuesday — Matthew 26:47-68 — Psalm 55:12-14, 20-21
- ☐ Wednesday — Matthew 26:69-27:20 — Daniel 2:26-28a
- ☐ Thursday — Matthew 27:21-44 — Isaiah 53:1-3, 5
- ☐ Friday — Matthew 27:45-28:10 — Psalm 16:8-10
- ☐ Weekend — Matthew 28:11- Mark 1:20 — 1 Chronicles 16:23-25

Week 8
- ☐ Monday — Mark 1:21-45 — Hosea 6:1-3
- ☐ Tuesday — Mark 2:1-22 — Isaiah 53:10-12
- ☐ Wednesday — Mark 2:23-3:27 — Isaiah 56:1-2
- ☐ Thursday — Mark 3:28-4:20 — Exodus 19:3-5
- ☐ Friday — Mark 4:21- 5:10 — Psalm 29:3-5, 7, 10
- ☐ Weekend — Mark 5:11-36 — 1 Samuel 17:42-47, 50

Week 9
- ☐ Monday — Mark 5:37-6:20 — Deuteronomy 1:42-45
- ☐ Tuesday — Mark : 6-21–44 — Psalm 107:8-9
- ☐ Wednesday — Mark 6:45-7:13 — Psalm 78:32-39
- ☐ Thursday — Mark 7:14-37 — Proverbs 6:12-19
- ☐ Friday — Mark 8:1-26 — Psalm 78:40-43
- ☐ Weekend — Mark 8:27-9:13 — Ecclesiastes 2:10-11

Week 10
- ☐ Monday — Mark 9:14-37 — Exodus 33:7-11
- ☐ Tuesday — Mark 9:38-10:16 — Genesis 39:6b-12
- ☐ Wednesday — Mark 10:17-41 — Psalm 58:11
- ☐ Thursday — Mark 10:42-11:14 — Genesis 22:1-2, 10-12
- ☐ Friday — Mark 11:15-12:12 — Psalm 145:18-19
- ☐ Weekend — Mark 12:13-31 — Psalm 140:1-8

Week 11
- ☐ Monday — Mark 12:32-13:10 — Exodus 36:3b-7
- ☐ Tuesday — Mark 13:11-37 — Daniel 11:33-35
- ☐ Wednesday — Mark 14:1-26 — Exodus 12:14, 25-27
- ☐ Thursday — Mark 14:27-52 — 1 Kings 8:54-59
- ☐ Friday — Mark 14:53-15:5 — Psalm 26:1-2
- ☐ Weekend — Mark 15:6-32 — Psalm 22:16-18

Week 12
- ☐ Monday — Mark 15:33-16:8 — Isaiah 35:7-10
- ☐ Tuesday — Mark 16:9-Luke 1:13 — Numbers 14:6-7, 9, 11, 20-24
- ☐ Wednesday — Luke 1:14-45 — Malachi 4:5-6
- ☐ Thursday — Luke 1:46-77 — Lamentations 3:21-26
- ☐ Friday — Luke 1:78-2:26 — Isaiah 12:2b-5a
- ☐ Weekend — Luke 2:27-52 — 1 Samuel 1:24-28

Week 13
- ☐ Monday — Luke 3:1-22 — Isaiah 40:6, 8, 9c-10
- ☐ Tuesday — Luke 3:23-38 — Isaiah 11:1-5
- ☐ Wednesday — Luke 4:1-30 — Isaiah 61:1-3a

	New Testament	*Old Testament*
WEEK 13 *continued*		
❏ Thursday	Luke 4:31-5:11	2 Kings 5:10-11a, 13-14
❏ Friday	Luke 5:12-35	Psalm 119:145-151
❏ Weekend	Luke 5:36-6:23	Psalm 37:10-13
WEEK 14		
❏ Monday	Luke 6:24-45	Jonah 4:1-2
❏ Tuesday	Luke 6:46-7:23	Psalm 18:46
❏ Wednesday	Luke 7:24-50	Job 11:4-6
❏ Thursday	Luke 8:1-21	Psalm 78:1-4
❏ Friday	Luke 8:22-48	Psalm 9:9
❏ Weekend	Luke 8:49-9:17	Job 12:7-10
WEEK 15		
❏ Monday	Luke 9:18-43a	Nehemiah 9:30-31
❏ Tuesday	Luke 9:43b-10:7	2 Chronicles 16:7-9b
❏ Wednesday	Luke 10:8-29	1 Kings 4:29-34
❏ Thursday	Luke 10:30 - 11:13	Proverbs 3:27-28
❏ Friday	Luke 11:14-36	Proverbs 4:25-27
❏ Weekend	Luke 11:37-12:7	Isaiah 51:12-13a
WEEK 16		
❏ Monday	Luke 12:8-34	Ecclesiastes 5:10-11
❏ Tuesday	Luke 12:35-56	Psalm 24:1-6
❏ Wednesday	Luke 12:57-13:21	Isaiah 5:7, 15-16
❏ Thursday	Luke 13:22-14:14	Proverbs 18:12
❏ Friday	Luke 14:15-15:10	Daniel 3:16-18
❏ Weekend	Luke 15:11-16:18	Ezekiel 33:15
WEEK 17		
❏ Monday	Luke 16:9-17:4	Psalm 139:23-24
❏ Tuesday	Luke 17:5-37	Genesis 19:12-13
❏ Wednesday	Luke 18:1-25	Jeremiah 9:23-24a
❏ Thursday	Luke 18:26-19:10	Jonah 3:4-5, 10
❏ Friday	Luke 19:11-40	Isaiah 3:10-11
❏ Weekend	Luke 19:41-20:19	Isaiah 1:10, 15b-16
WEEK 18		
❏ Monday	Luke 20:20-47	Micah 2:1-3
❏ Tuesday	Luke 21:1-28	Exodus 4:10-11, 14-15
❏ Wednesday	Luke 21:29-22:20	Psalm 119:57-60
❏ Thursday	Luke 22:21-53	Psalm 143: 9-10
❏ Friday	Luke 22:54-23:12	Genesis 27:35-37, 41
❏ Weekend	Luke 23:13-43	Isaiah 30:15, 18
WEEK 19		
❏ Monday	Luke 23:44-24:12	Isaiah 42:1-4, 6-7b
❏ Tuesday	Luke 24:13-53	Isaiah 40:9-10a
❏ Wednesday	John 1:1-28	Isaiah 9:2, 6
❏ Thursday	John 1:29-51	Isaiah 53:6-8
❏ Friday	John 2:1-25	Psalm 101:6-8
❏ Weekend	John 3:1-30	Isaiah 59:15b-17

	New Testament	*Old Testament*
WEEK 20		
☐ Monday	John 3:31-4:26	Jeremiah 2:12-13, 18-19
☐ Tuesday	John 4:27-54	2 Chronicles 20:20-22
☐ Wednesday	John 5:1-29	Psalm 34:21-22
☐ Thursday	John 5:30-6:15	Genesis 49:9-10
☐ Friday	John 6:16-40	1 Chronicles 16:8-12
☐ Weekend	John 6:41-71	Numbers 14:1-4
WEEK 21		
☐ Monday	John 7:1-31	1 Kings 22:7-8
☐ Tuesday	John 7:32-8:11	Proverbs 20:9
☐ Wednesday	John 8:12-41	Psalm 2:10-12
☐ Thursday	John 8:42-9:12	Numbers 25:10-12
☐ Friday	John 9:13-41	Psalm 119:17-24
☐ Weekend	John 10:1-33	Isaiah 40:11
WEEK 22		
☐ Monday	John 10:34-11:27	Psalm 40:1-3
☐ Tuesday	John 11:28-57	1 Kings 17:21-22, 24
☐ Wednesday	John 12:1-26	Psalm 10:12-15
☐ Thursday	John 12:27-13:5	Numbers 11:10-11, 13b-16a, 18, 21-23
☐ Friday	John 13:6-35	Exodus 20:3, 5a, 7a, 8, 12a, 13-17a
☐ Weekend	John 13:36-14:26	Deuteronomy 11:13-14
WEEK 23		
☐ Monday	John 14:27-15:27	Psalm 51:10-13
☐ Tuesday	John 16:1-28	Psalm 37:3-6
☐ Wednesday	John 16:29-17:20	Psalm 91:1-8
☐ Thursday	John 17:21-18:18	Psalm 133:1-3
☐ Friday	John 18:19-19:3	Psalm 117:1-2
☐ Weekend	John 19:4-27	Jeremiah 27:4-7
WEEK 24		
☐ Monday	John 19:28-20:9	Psalm 47:1-9
☐ Tuesday	John 20:10-21:3	Judges 6:36-40
☐ Wednesday	John 21:4-25	Numbers 27:15-17
☐ Thursday	Acts 1:1-26	Psalm 96:12-13
☐ Friday	Acts 2:1-28	Isaiah 44:1-3
☐ Weekend	Acts 2:29-3:10	Hosea 6:1-3b
WEEK 25		
☐ Monday	Acts 3:11-4:12	Isaiah 28:16-17
☐ Tuesday	Acts 4:13-37	Isaiah 43:4-7
☐ Wednesday	Acts 5:1-26	Joshua 7:20-21, 24-25
☐ Thursday	Acts 5:27-6:7	Isaiah 46:8-11
☐ Friday	Acts 6:8-7:16	Psalm 105:1-4
☐ Weekend	Acts 7:17-42a	Psalm 105:28-37
WEEK 26		
☐ Monday	Acts 7:42b-8:1	2 Chronicles 24:18-21
☐ Tuesday	Acts 8:2-25	Numbers 16:1a, 2-3, 8-9, 28-30

	New Testament	*Old Testament*
WEEK 26 continued		
☐ Wednesday	Acts 8:26-9:9	Nehemiah 8:7-12
☐ Thursday	Acts 9:10-35	1 Samuel 16:12c-13
☐ Friday	Acts 9:36-10:23a	1 Kings 9:1-3
☐ Weekend	Acts 10:23b-48	Isaiah 1:18-20
WEEK 27		
☐ Monday	Acts 11:1-30	Proverbs 22:9
☐ Tuesday	Acts 12:1-25	Exodus 14:29-31
☐ Wednesday	Acts 13:1-25	Exodus 4:29-31
☐ Thursday	Acts 13:26-52	Jeremiah 15:16
☐ Friday	Acts 14:1-28	Proverbs 3:5-7
☐ Weekend	Acts 15:1-21	Isaiah 45:22
WEEK 28		
☐ Monday	Acts 15:22-16:10	Proverbs 25:11
☐ Tuesday	Acts 16:11-34	2 Kings 4:8-10
☐ Wednesday	Acts 16:35-17:15	Isaiah 55:10-11
☐ Thursday	Acts 17:16-18:4	Genesis 2:4-7
☐ Friday	Acts 18:5-28	Psalm 121:5-8
☐ Weekend	Acts 19:1-22	2 Kings 11:17-18
WEEK 29		
☐ Monday	Acts 19:23-20:6	Psalms 124:2-3, 6-8
☐ Tuesday	Acts 20:7-38	1 Kings 18:40
☐ Wednesday	Acts 21:1-25	Exodus 32:7, 26-27, 29
☐ Thursday	Acts 21:26-22:5	Ezekiel 2:3-5
☐ Friday	Acts 22:6-29	Psalm 33:8-12
☐ Weekend	Acts 22:30-23:22	Psalm 75:1-3
WEEK 30		
☐ Monday	Acts 23:23-24:16	Jeremiah 22:15b-16
☐ Tuesday	Acts 24:17-25:12	Genesis 3:7-10
☐ Wednesday	Acts 25:13-26:8	2 Samuel 22:21-25
☐ Thursday	Acts 26:9-32	Exodus 15:11-14a
☐ Friday	Acts 27:1-26	Joshua 1:6-8
☐ Weekend	Acts 27:27-28:11a	Jonah 1:15-16
WEEK 31		
☐ Monday	Acts 28:11b-31	Genesis 24:28, 29a, 30b-32a
☐ Tuesday	Romans 1:1-27	Psalm 19:1-4a
☐ Wednesday	Romans 1:28-2:16	Proverbs 15:9-11
☐ Thursday	Romans 2:17-3:18	Jeremiah 7:3, 5-6
☐ Friday	Romans 3:19-4:12	Psalm 32:10-11
☐ Weekend	Romans 4:13-5:11	Isaiah 63:7-9c
WEEK 32		
☐ Monday	Romans 5:12-6:14	Jeremiah 18:11-12
☐ Tuesday	Romans 6:15-7:13	Deuteronomy 7:6-8
☐ Wednesday	Romans 7:14-8:17	Joshua 24:14-15
☐ Thursday	Romans 8:18-39	Isaiah 59:15b-17, 21
☐ Friday	Romans 9:1-29	Isaiah 1:9
☐ Weekend	Romans 9:30-10:21	Isaiah 65:1

	New Testament	*Old Testament*

Week 33
- ❏ Monday — Romans 11:1-21 — Ezekiel 18:21-23
- ❏ Tuesday — Romans 11:22-12:8 — 1 Samuel 15:22
- ❏ Wednesday — Romans 12:9-13:14 — Psalm 37:21, 26
- ❏ Thursday — Romans 14:1-15:3 — Proverbs 12:14
- ❏ Friday — Romans 15:4-29 — Psalm 33:20-22
- ❏ Weekend — Romans 15:30-16:27 — Ezekiel 13:3, 7

Week 34
- ❏ Monday — 1 Corinthians 1:1-25 — Isaiah 44:24b-26a
- ❏ Tuesday — 1 Corinthians 1:26-2:16 — Job 28:20-28
- ❏ Wednesday — 1 Corinthians 3:1-4:5 — Psalm 118:22
- ❏ Thursday — 1 Corinthians 4:6-5:8 — Deuteronomy 17:2, 4b-5, 12
- ❏ Friday — 1 Corinthians 5:9-6:20 — Proverbs 6:27-29
- ❏ Weekend — 1 Corinthians 7:1-24 — Malachi 2:15-16b

Week 35
- ❏ Monday — 1 Corinthians 7:25-8:8 — Jeremiah 1:4-5; 9-10, 16:1-2
- ❏ Tuesday — 1 Corinthians 8:9-9:18 — Amos 2:11-14
- ❏ Wednesday — 1 Corinthians 9:19-10:22 — John 2:3-10
- ❏ Thursday — 1 Corinthians 10:23-11:22 — 1 Samuel 2:12, 30-31
- ❏ Friday — 1 Corinthians 11:23-12:13 — Deuteronomy 34:9
- ❏ Weekend — 1 Corinthians 12:14-13:13 — Ruth 2:14-16

Week 36
- ❏ Monday — 1 Corinthians 14:1-25 — 2 Kings 23:15-16
- ❏ Tuesday — 1 Corinthians 14:26-15:11 — Psalm 47:5-8
- ❏ Wednesday — 1 Corinthians 15:12-44a — Daniel 12:2-3
- ❏ Thursday — 1 Corinthians 15:44b-16:24 — Psalm 35:1, 7
- ❏ Friday — 2 Corinthians 1:1-17 — Psalm 56:1-4
- ❏ Weekend — 2 Corinthians 1:18-3:3 — Genesis 50:16-17, 19-21

Week 37
- ❏ Monday — 2 Corinthians 3:4-4:15 — Job 24:13, 23-24
- ❏ Tuesday — 2 Corinthians 4:16-6:2 — Psalm 24:3-6
- ❏ Wednesday — 2 Corinthians 6:3-7:7 — Proverbs 4:14-15
- ❏ Thursday — 2 Corinthians 7:8-8:15 — Ezra 10:1-3b
- ❏ Friday — 2 Corinthians 8:16-9:15 — Proverbs 28:27
- ❏ Weekend — 2 Corinthians 10:1-11:4 — 2 Chronicles 20:20-22

Week 38
- ❏ Monday — 2 Corinthians 11:5-33 — Exodus 1:22
- ❏ Tuesday — 2 Corinthians 12:1-13:4 — 1 Samuel 30:6b, 8
- ❏ Wednesday — 2 Corinthians 13:5-Galatians 1:21 — 1 Samuel 9:17
- ❏ Thursday — Galatians 1:22-2:21 — Proverbs 21:13
- ❏ Friday — Galatians 3:1-20 — Genesis 22:15-17a
- ❏ Weekend — Galatians 3:21-4:20 — Isaiah 64:8-9

Week 39
- ❏ Monday — Galatians 4:21-5:15 — Genesis 21:8-12
- ❏ Tuesday — Galatians 5:16-6:18 — Ecclesiastes 2:26
- ❏ Wednesday — Ephesians 1:1-2:3 — Job 42:8b-9

	New Testament	*Old Testament*
WEEK 39 *continued*		
❏ Thursday	Ephesians 2:4-3:6	Micah 7:18-19a
❏ Friday	Ephesians 3:7-4:16	Psalm 136:1, 4
❏ Weekend	Ephesians 4:17-5:14	Proverbs 30:15-16
WEEK 40		
❏ Monday	Ephesians 5:15-6:4	Song of Solomon 2:16-17
❏ Tuesday	Ephesians 6:5-24	Job 1:6-10
❏ Wednesday	Philippians 1:1-2:4	Micah 6:8
❏ Thursday	Philippians 2:5-30	Proverbs 20:3
❏ Friday	Philippians 3:1-21	Psalm 42:1-2
❏ Weekend	Philippians 4:1-23	Psalm 55:22
WEEK 41		
❏ Monday	Colossians 1:1-23	Isaiah 41:2a-b, 4
❏ Tuesday	Colossians 1:24-2:15	Psalm 40:1-4
❏ Wednesday	Colossians 2:16-3:17	Leviticus 20:7-8, 26
❏ Thursday	Colossians 3:18-4:18	Proverbs 6:20-22
❏ Friday	1 Thessalonians 1:1-2:16	Deuteronomy 7:7-8a
❏ Weekend	1 Thessalonians 2:17-4:12	Leviticus 22:31-33
WEEK 42		
❏ Monday	1 Thessalonians 4:13-5:28	Job 19:25-27
❏ Tuesday	2 Thessalonians 1:1-2:12	Isaiah 1:27-28
❏ Wednesday	2 Thessalonians 2:13-3:18	Proverbs 31:10-16
❏ Thursday	1 Timothy 1:1-20	Isaiah 55:7
❏ Friday	1 Timothy 2:1-3:13	Deuteronomy 4:34-38
❏ Weekend	1 Timothy 3:14-4:16	2 Kings 23:3, 24-25
WEEK 43		
❏ Monday	1 Timothy 5:1-25	2 Samuel 12:7, 9, 13-14
❏ Tuesday	1 Timothy 6:1-21	Ecclesiastes 5:19-20
❏ Wednesday	2 Timothy 1:1-2:13	Deuteronomy 4:9-10
❏ Thursday	2 Timothy 2:14-3:11	Psalm 101:1-5
❏ Friday	2 Timothy 3:12-4:22	Nehemiah 8:8, 14-15
❏ Weekend	Titus 1:1-2:8	Malachi 2:7-9
WEEK 44		
❏ Monday	Titus 2:9-3:15	Daniel 6:21-22, 25-27
❏ Tuesday	Philemon 1-25	Genesis 41:39-40, 42-43
❏ Wednesday	Hebrews 1:1-2:4	Psalm 86:11-13
❏ Thursday	Hebrews 2:5-3:6	Ezekiel 37:22, 23b-28
❏ Friday	Hebrews 3:7-4:13	Numbers 14:8-9, 20-23
❏ Weekend	Hebrews 4:14-6:8	Exodus 28:1-3
WEEK 45		
❏ Monday	Hebrews 6:9-7:10	Joshua 23:5-6, 14-16
❏ Tuesday	Hebrews 7:11-8:6	Jeremiah 31:33
❏ Wednesday	Hebrews 8:7-9:12	Isaiah 53:10-11
❏ Thursday	Hebrews 9:13-10:10	Leviticus 16:15, 17b, 34
❏ Friday	Hebrews 10:11-39	Amos 5:14
❏ Weekend	Hebrews 11:1-22	Genesis 15:5-6

	New Testament	*Old Testament*
Week 46		
☐ Monday	Hebrews 11:23-12:6	Job 5:17-18
☐ Tuesday	Hebrews 12:7-29	2 Samuel 24:10, 15a, 17-19, 25b
☐ Wednesday	Hebrews 13:1-25	Deuteronomy 10:12b-13, 16, 18-21
☐ Thursday	James 1:1-27	1 Kings 3:10-13
☐ Friday	James 2:1-26	Obadiah 13-14
☐ Weekend	James 3:1-4:10	Proverbs 18:20-21
Week 47		
☐ Monday	James 4:11-5:20	Esther 4:15-16
☐ Tuesday	1 Peter 1:1-21	Zechariah 13:9
☐ Wednesday	1 Peter 1:22-2:17	Daniel 3:28-29
☐ Thursday	1 Peter 2:18-3:12	Genesis 26:26-31
☐ Friday	1 Peter 3:13-4:11	Psalm 71:12-16
☐ Weekend	1 Peter 4:12-5:14	1 Kings 17:2-4, 6-9
Week 48		
☐ Monday	2 Peter 1:1-21	Proverbs 1:1, 3, 7
☐ Tuesday	2 Peter 2:1-22	Isaiah 56:11
☐ Wednesday	2 Peter 3:1-18	Psalm 22:3-8
☐ Thursday	1 John 1:1-2:14	Job 38:15a
☐ Friday	1 John 2:15-3:10	Ecclesiastes 2:10-11
☐ Weekend	1 John 3:11-4:12	2 Samuel 9:3, 5-7
Week 49		
☐ Monday	1 John 4:13-5:21	Psalm 66:19-20
☐ Tuesday	2 John 1-3 John 15	Deuteronomy 31:7-8
☐ Wednesday	Jude 1-13	Isaiah 13:6-11
☐ Thursday	Jude 14-25	Jeremiah 9:23-24
☐ Friday	Revelation 1:1-20	Isaiah 48:12-13
☐ Weekend	Revelation 2:1-17	Jeremiah 3:12
Week 50		
☐ Monday	Revelation 2:18-3:6	Deuteronomy 10:12
☐ Tuesday	Revelation 3:7-4:5	Daniel 12:1-3
☐ Wednesday	Revelation 4:6-6:2	Isaiah 6:1-5
☐ Thursday	Revelation 6:3-7:8	Nahum 1:2a, 5-6a
☐ Friday	Revelation 7:9-8:13	Isaiah 61:10
☐ Weekend	Revelation 9:1-10:4	Joel 2:1b, 10-12
Week 51		
☐ Monday	Revelation 10:5-11:14	1 Kings 17:1; 18:1-2
☐ Tuesday	Revelation 11:15-12:12	Daniel 7:21-22
☐ Wednesday	Revelation 12:13-13:18	Daniel 11:32-35
☐ Thursday	Revelation 14:1-20	Jeremiah 25:15-17, 26b
☐ Friday	Revelation 15:1-16:11	Deuteronomy 32:19-20, 23-24
☐ Weekend	Revelation 16:12-17:8	Ezekiel 38:18-23
Week 52		
☐ Monday	Revelation 17:9-18:10	Genesis 19:15
☐ Tuesday	Revelation 18:11-24	Jeremiah 51:25-26, 36a
☐ Wednesday	Revelation 19:1-16	Exodus 15:11-13, 17-18
☐ Thursday	Revelation 19:17-20:15	Ezekiel 39:1, 4-8
☐ Friday	Revelation 21:1-27	Zechariah 2:10-13
☐ Weekend	Revelation 22:1-21	Psalm 46:4-5a

ACKNOWLEDGMENTS

Alcorn, Randy C. taken from *Sexual Temptation*. © 1989 by Randy Alcorn. Used by permission of InterVarsity Press, P.O. Box 1400, Downers Grove, IL 60515.

Anderson, Lynn, *Finding the Heart to Go On*, Here's Life Publishers, San Bernadino, CA, © 1991.

Arnold, Duane W.H., taken from the book *Prayers of the Martyrs*. Copyright ©1991 by Duane W. H. Arnold. Used by permission of Zondervan Publishing House.

Augsburger, David W., taken from *Freedom of Forgiveness*, Copyright © 1970, 1988. Moody Bible Institute of Chicago. Moody Press. Used by permission.

Avila, St. Theresa of, from the book *A Life of Prayer*, copyright 1983 by Multnomah Press. Published by Multnomah Press, Portland, OR 97206. Used by permission.

Babcock, Maltbie, *This Is My Father's World* in *The Hymnal for Worship and Celebration*, copyright © 1986, Word Music, Waco, TX.

Barna, George, *The Frog in the Kettle*, copyright © 1990 by Regal Books, a division of Gospel Light Publications. Used by permission.

Baxter, J. Sidlow, taken from the book *Awake My Heart*. Copyright © 1959 by J. Sidlow Baxter. Used by permission of the Zondervan Publishing House.

Beals, Art, *Beyond Hunger*, copyright © 1985. Multnomah Press, Portland, OR 97266.

Beckwith, Mary, *Still Moments*, copyright © 1989 by Regal Books, a division of Gospel Light Publications. Used by permission.

Blue, Ron, *Master Your Money*, copyright © 1986, Thomas Nelson Publishers, Nashville, TN.

Boice, James Montgomery, taken from *The Parables of Jesus*. Copyright © 1983. Moody Bible Institute of Chicago. Moody Press. Used by permission.

Bridges, Jerry, *The Practice of Godliness*, copyright © 1983 by Jerry Bridges, NavPress, Colorado Springs, CO.

Bridges, Jerry, *The Pursuit of Holiness*, copyright © 1978 by the Navigators, NavPress, Colorado Springs, CO.

Bright, Bill, *Promises—a Daily Guide to Supernatural Living*, Here's Life Publishers, San Bernadino, CA, © 1983.

Bright, Bill, *The Secret: How to Live with Purpose and Power*, Here's Life Publishers, San Bernadino, CA, © 1989.

Briscoe, Jill, *Running on Empty*, copyright © 1988, Word, Inc., Dallas, TX.

Bruce, F. F., taken from *The Hard Sayings of Jesus*, © 1983 by F. F. Bruce. Used by permission of InterVarsity Press, P.O. Box 1400, Downers Grove, IL 60515. Worldwide permission granted by Hodder & Stoughton Limited, England.

Bryant, Al, (Compiler) *Day By Day With C. H. Spurgeon*, copyright © 1980, Word, Inc., Dallas, TX.

Bryant, Al, *Keep in Touch*, copyright © 1981, Word, Inc., Dallas, TX.

Buechner, Frederick, excerpt from *Wishful Thinking*. Copyright © 1973 by Frederick Buechner. Reprinted by permission of HarperCollins Publishers.

Calkins, Ruth Harms, from *Tell Me Again Lord, I Forget*, © 1974. Used by permission of Tyndale House Publishers, Inc. All rights reserved.

Campolo, Anthony, *The Kingdom of God is a Party*, copyright © 1990, Word, Inc., Dallas, TX.

Campolo, Anthony, *Who Switched the Price Tags?*, copyright © 1986, Word, Inc., Dallas, TX.

Chapian, Marie, *Discovering Joy*, Bethany House Publishers, © 1990.

Chisholm, Thomas O. (Words) and Runyan, William M. (Music), *Great Is Thy Faithfulness* in *The Hymnal for Worship and Celebration*, copyright © 1923. Renewal 1951 by Hope Publishing Co., Carol Stream, IL 60188. All rights reserved. Used by permission.

Crabb, Rachael, *The Personal Touch*, copyright © 1990 by Rachael Crabb and Raeann Hart, NavPress, Colorado Springs, CO.

Evans, Anthony T., taken from *America's Only Hope*. Copyright © 1990. Moody Bible Institute of Chicago. Moody Press. Used by permission.

Fickett, Harold L., *Walking What You're Talking (Principles of James)*, copyright © 1988 by Regal Books, a division of Gospel Light Publications. Used by permission.

Finney, Charles G., *God's Love for a Sinning World*. © 1966 by Kregel Publications: Grand Rapids, Michigan. Used by permission.

Finney, Charles G., *Principles of Consecration*, Bethany House Publishers, © 1990.

Finney, Charles Grandison, *Principles of Devotion*, Bethany House Publishers, 1987.

Finney, Charles G., *Victory Over the World*. © 1966 by Kregel Publications: Grand Rapids, Michigan Used by permission.

Fletcher, William M., *The Second Greatest Commandment*. Copyright © 1983. NavPress, Colorado Springs, CO. (Dr. William M. Fletcher is Minister-at-Large, Rocky Mountain Conservative Baptist Association.)

Foster, Richard J., excerpts from *Celebration of Discipline*. Copyright © 1978 by Richard J. Foster. Reprinted by permission of HarperCollins Publishers.

Foster, Richard J., excerpts from *Money, Sex and Power*. Copyright © 1985 by Richard J. Foster. Reprinted by permission of HarperCollins Publishers.

Fullham, Terry L., *Thirsting*, copyright © 1989, Thomas Nelson Publishers, Nashville, TN.

Gaither, Gloria, *We Have This Moment*, copyright © 1988, Word, Inc., Dallas, TX.

Geisler, Norman L., (Editor), *What Augustine Says*, Baker Book House, © 1982.

Gillham, Bill, *Lifetime Guarantee*, Wolgemuth & Hyatt, Publishers, Inc., Used by permission.

Graham, Billy, *Answers to Life's Problems*, copyright © 1960, Word, Inc., Dallas, TX.

Graham, Billy, *Approaching Hoofbeats*, copyright © 1983, Word, Inc., Dallas, TX.

Graham, Billy, *The Holy Spirit*, copyright © 1978, 1988, Word, Inc., Dallas, TX.

Graham, Billy, *Unto the Hills: A Devotional Treasury from Billy Graham*, copyright © 1986, Word, Inc., Dallas, TX.

Gregory, Joel C., *Growing Pains of the Soul*, copyright © 1987, Word, Inc., Dallas, TX.

Guiness, Os, taken from *The Devil's Gauntlet*. © 1989 by Os Guiness. Used by permission of InterVarsity Press, P.O. Box 1400, Downers Grove, IL 60515.

Halverson, Richard C., *No Greater Power*, copyright © 1986, Multnomah Press, Portland, OR 97266

Harris, Madalene, *Climbing Higher*, Here's Life Publishers, San Bernadino, CA, © 1989.

Hayford, Jack, from *Daybreak*, © 1984. Used by permission of Tyndale House Publishers Inc. All rights reserved.

Hendrichson, Walter A., Reprinted by permission from *Disciples are Made—Not Born*. Published by Victor Books and © 1974 by SP Publications, Inc., Wheaton, IL.

Hendricks, Howard G. and Jeanne W., from the book *Footprints*, copyright © 1981, Multnomah Press, Portland, OR 97266. (Howard Hendricks is a distinguished professor at Dallas Theological Seminary; Jeanne Hendricks is an author, mother of four, and grandmother of six.)

Hession, Roy, from *The Calvary Road*, copyright 1952, Christian Literature Crusade, London (Ft. Washington, PA and Alresford, Hants: Christian Literature Crusade). Used by permission.

Hocking, David L., from the book *The Coming World Leader*, copyright 1988 by Calvary Communications, Inc. Published by Multnomah Press, Portland, OR 97266. Used by permissio

Hughes, R. Kent, taken from *Ephesians*, copyright 1990. Used with permission by Good News Publishers/Crossway Books, Wheaton, IL.

Hybels, Bill, *Seven Wonders of the Spiritual World*, copyright © 1988, Word, Inc., Dallas, TX.

Hybels, Bill, taken from *Too Busy Not to Pray*. © 1988 by Bill Hybels. Used by permission of InterVarsity Press, P.O. Box 1400, Downers, Grove, IL 60515.

Jeremiah, David and Carlson, Carole C., *Escape the Coming Night*, copyright © 1990, Word, Inc., Dallas, TX.

Johnson, Elliott and Schierbaum, Al, *Our Great and Awesome God: Meditations for Athletes*. Wolgemuth & Hyatt, Publishers, Inc. Used by permission.

Keller, W. Phillip, *A Gardener Looks at the Fruits of the Spirit*, copyright © 1986, Word, Inc., Dallas, T

Keller, W. Phillip, *Salt for Society*, copyright © 1981, Word., Inc., Dallas, TX.

Keller, W. Phillip, *Songs of My Soul*, copyright © 1989, Word, Inc., Dallas, TX.

Keller, W. Phillip, *Taming Tension*, Baker Book House, © 1979.

Kempis, Thomas A., taken from *The Imitation of Christ*. Copyright © 1984. Moody Bible Institute o Chicago. Moody Press. Used by permission.

Kroll, Woodrow Michael, *Early in the Morning, Book Two*. Used by permission of Loizeaux Brothers, Inc., Neptune, New Jersey.

Lake, Vicki, reprinted by permission from *Firming Up Your Flabby Faith*. Published by Victor Books and © 1990 by SP Publications, Inc., Wheaton, IL.

Larson, Bruce, reprinted from *A Call to Holy Living*, copyright © 1988 Augsburg Publishing House. Used by permission of Augsburg Fortress.

Lee, Richard, *The Unfailing Promise*, copyright © 1988, Word, Inc., Dallas, TX.

Lockerbie, Jeanette, taken from *Springtime of Faith*. Copyright © 1990. Moody Bible Institute of Chicago. Moody Press. Used by permission.

Lockyer, Herbert, *Satan: His Person and Power*, copyright © 1980, Word, Inc., Dallas, TX.

Lucado, Max, *The Applause of Heaven*, copyright © 1990, Word, Inc., Dallas, TX.

Lucado, Max, from the book *God Came Near*, copyright © 1987 by Max Lucado. Published by Multnomah Press, Portland, OR 97266. Used by permission.

Lucado, Max, from *On the Anvil*, © 1985. Used by permission of Tyndale House Publishers, Inc. All rights reserved.

Luther, Martin, *A Mighty Fortress Is Our God* in *The Hymnal for Worship and Celebration*, © 1986, Word Music, Waco, TX.

MacArthur, John Jr., taken from the book *The Gospel According to Jesus*. Copyright © 1988 by John F. MacArthur, Jr. Used by permission of Zondervan Publishing House.

MacDonald, George, *Knowing the Heart of God*, Bethany House Publishers, © 1990.

MacDonald, Gordon, *Ordering Your Private World*, copyright © 1984, 1985, Thomas Nelson Publishers, Nashville, TN.

MacDonald, Gordon, *Rebuilding Your Broken World*, copyright © 1988, 1990, Thomas Nelson Publishers, Nashville, TN.

McClung, Floyd, *Holiness and the Spirit of the Age*. Copyright © 1990 by Harvest House Publishers, Eugene, OR 97402.

McClung, Floyd, taken from *Wholehearted*. © 1988, 1990 by Floyd McClung. Used by permission of InterVarsity Pres, P.O. Box 1400, Downers Grove, IL 60515. Worldwide permission granted by HarperCollins Publishers, London, England.

McCullough, Donald W., taken from *Finding Happiness in the Most Unlikely Places*. © 1990 by Donald W. McCullough. Used by permission of InterVarsity Press, P.O. Box 1400, Downers, Grove, IL 60515.

McKenna, David, from *Practical Christianity*; LaVonne Neff, Ron Beers, Bruce Barton, Linda Taylor, Dave Veerman, and Jim Galvin (Compilers and Editors), © 1987 by Youth for Christ/USA. Used by permission of Tyndale House Publishers. All rights reserved.

Magdalen, Margaret, taken from *Jesus, Man of Prayer*. © 1987 by Sister Margaret Magdalen. Used by permission of InterVarsity Press, P.O. Box 1400, Downers Grove, IL 60515. Worldwide permission granted by Hodder & Stoughton Limited, England.

Mains, David R., *The Sense of His Presence*, copyright © 1988, Word, Inc., Dallas, TX.

Mains, Karen Burton, taken from the book *You Are What You Say*. Copyright © 1988 by Karen Burton Mains. Used by permission of the Zondervan Publishing House.

Merritt, James Gregory, reprinted by permission from *God's Prescription for a Healthy Christian*. Published by Victor Books and © 1990 by SP Publications, Inc., Wheaton, IL.

Meyer, F.B., from *Devotional Commentary* by F. B. Meyer (1989) Tyndale house Publishers, Inc. Used by permission. All rights reserved.

Meyer, F. B., taken from *Our Daily Walk*. Copyright © 1951, 1972 by the Zondervan Publishing House. Used by permission.

Miley, Jeanie, *Creative Silence: Keys to the Deeper Life*, copyright © 1989, Word, Inc., Dallas, TX.

Mitchell, John G., from the book *An Everlasting Love*, copyright © 1982 by Multnomah Press. Published by Multnomah Press, Portland, OR 97206. Used by permission.

Moody, D. L., taken from *The Way to God and How to Find It*. Copyright © 1983. Moody Bible Institute of Chicago. Moody Press. Used by permission.

Morley, Patrick, *I Surrender*. Wolgemuth & Hyatt, Publishers, Inc. Used by permission.

Mote, Edward, *The Solid Rock* in *The Hymnal for Worship and Celebration*, copyright © 1986, Word Music, Waco, TX.

Muggeridge, Malcolm, from *The End of Christendom*, copyright © 1980 by William B. Eerdmans Publishing Co., pp. 51-54. Used by permission.

Muggeridge, Malcolm, *A Twentieth Century Testimony*, copyright © 1978, Thomas Nelson Publishers, Nashville, TN.

Murray, Andrew, from *Abide in Christ* (Ft. Washington, PA: Christian Literature Crusade).

Murray, Andrew, *The Believer's Secret of Living Like Christ*, Bethany House Publishers, © 1985.

Murray, Andrew, *The Believer's Secret of Waiting on God*, Bethany House Publishers, © 1986.

Murray, Andrew, *The Believer's Secret of Waiting on God*, Bethany House Publishers, © 1986.

Murray, Andrew, taken from *The True Vine*. Copyright © 1983. Moody Bible Institute of Chicago. Moody Press. Used by permission.

Murray, Andrew, and Edwards, Jonathan; Parkhurst, Louis Gifford (Compiler and Editor), *The Believer's Secret of Christian Love*, Bethany House Publishers, © 1990.

Murray, Andrew, and Finney, Charles G.; Parkhurst, L. G. (Compiler and Editor), *The Believer's Secret of Spiritual Power*, Bethany House Publishers, ©, 1987.

Myers, Warren and Ruth, *Pray: How to Be Effective in Prayer*, copyright © 1983, Navpress, Colorado Springs, Colorado.

Oatman, Johnson Jr., *Count Your Blessings* in *The Hymnal for Worship and Celebration*, copyright © Word Music, Waco, Texas.

Ogilvie, Lloyd, *Enjoying God*, copyright © 1989, Word, Inc., Dallas, Texas.

Ogilvie, Lloyd John, taken from *Silent Strength for My Life*. Copyright © 1990 by Harvest House Publishers, Eugene, OR 97402. Used by permission.

Ortlund, Anne, *Disclpines of the Home*, copyright © Word, Inc., Dallas, Texas.

Packer, J. I., taken from *Knowing God*. © 1973 by J. I. Packer. Used by permission of InterVarsity Press, P.O. Box 1400, Downers Grove, IL 60515. Worldwide permission granted by Hodder & Stoughton Limited, England.

Packer, James and Watson, Jean, reprinted from *Your Father Loves You*, © 1986. Used by permission of Harold Shaw Publishers, Wheaton, IL. Worldwide permission granted bv Hodder & Stoughton Limited, England.

Palau, Luis, reprinted by permission from *Time to Stop Pretending*. Published by Victor Books and © 1985 by SP Publications, Inc., Wheaton, IL.

Pinnock, Clark H., from *Practical Christianity;* LaVonne Neff, Ron Beers, Bruce Barton, Linda Taylor, Dave Veerman, and Jim Galvin (Compilers and Editors), © 1987 by Youth for Christ/USA. Used by permission of Tyndale House Publishers. All rights reserved.

Pippert, Rebecca Manley, taken from *Out of the Saltshaker and Into the World*. © 1979 by Inter-Varsity Christian Fellowship of the USA. Used by permission of InterVarsity Press, P.O. Box 1400, Downers Grove, IL 60515.

Reid, David, *Devotions for Growing Christians*. Used by permission of Loizeaux Brothers, Inc. Neptune, New Jersey.

Ryrie, Charles C., reprinted by permission from *The Final Countdown*. Published by Victor Books and © 1982 by SP Publications, Inc., Wheaton, IL.

Sanders, J. Oswald, taken from *Enjoying Intimacy With God*. Copyright © 1980. Moody Bible Institute of Chicago. Moody Press. Used by permission.

Sanders, J. Oswald, taken from *Just Like Us*. Copyright © 1978. Moody Bible Institute of Chicago. Moody Press. Used by permission.

Sanders, J. Oswald, taken from *Shoe Leather Commitment*. Copyright © 1990. Moody Bible Institu of Chicago. Moody Press. Used by permission.

Schaeffer, Edith, from the book *Affliction*, copyright G 1978 by Edith Schaeffer. Used by permission of Fleming H. Revell Company.

Schaeffer, Edith, *Common Sense Christian Living*, Copyright 1983, Thomas Nelson Publishers, Nashville, TN.

Schmidt, Thomas E., taken from the book *Trying to Be Good*. Copyright © 1990 by Thomas E. Schmidt. Used by permission of the Zondervan Publishing House.

Senter, Ruth, taken from *The Attributes of God*. Copyright © 1987. Moody Bible Institute of Chicago. Moody Press. Used by permission.

Senter, Ruth, *Longing for Love,* copyright © 1991 by Ruth Senter, NavPress, Colorado Springs, Colorado.

Senter, Ruth, taken from the book *Startled by Silence*. Copyright © 1986 by Ruth Senter. Used by permission of the Zondervan Publishing House.

Shaw, Luci, reprinted from *Postcard from the Shore,* © 1985 by Luci Shaw. Used by permission of Harold Shaw Publishers, Wheaton, IL.

Sherman, Doug and Hendricks, William, *How to Succeed Where It Really Counts,* copyright © 1989 by Doug Sherman and William Hendricks, NavPress, Colorado Springs, Colorado.

Sider, Ronald J., *Rich Christians in an Age of Hunger,* copyright © 1990, Word, Inc., Dallas, Texas.

Simpson, A. B., taken from the book *Days of Heaven on Earth*. Copyright © 1984 by Christian Publications. Used by permission of the Zondervan Publishing House.

Smith, F. LaGard, *The Daily Gospels* (formerly *The Intimate Jesus*). Copyright © 1988 by Harvest House Publishers, Eugene, OR 97402.

Smith, Hannah Whitall, from the book *The Christian's Secret of a Happy Life*. Copyright © 1952 by Fleming H. Revell Company. Used by permission of Fleming H. Revell Company.

Sollenberger, Lucille Fern, *My Daily Appointment with God,* copyright © 1988, Word, Inc., Dallas, Texas.

Sproul, R. C., from *Effective Prayer,* © 1984. Used by permission of Tyndale House Publishers, Inc. All rights reserved.

Sproul, R. C., from *The Holiness of God,* © 1985. Used by permission of Tyndale House Publishers, Inc. All rights reserved.

Sproul, R. C., *One Holy Passion,* copyright © 1987, Thomas Nelson Publishers, Nashville, TN.

Spurgeon, C. H., taken from *All of Grace*. Copyright © 1984. Moody Bible Institute of Chicago. Moody Press. Used by permission.

Spurgeon, Charles H., taken from *Faith's Checkbook*. Copyright © 1987. Moody Bible Institute of Chicago. Moody Press. Used by permission.

Spurgeon, Charles H., *Morning and Evening,* copyright © 1991, Hendrickson Publishers, Inc. Peabody, MA.

Spurgeon, C. H., reprinted from *The Quotable Spurgeon,* © 1990 by Harold Shaw Publishers, Wheaton, IL. Used by permission.

Stamm, Mildred, taken from the book *Meditation Moments for Women*. Copyright © 1967 by the Zondervan Publishing House. Used by permission.

Stamm, Millie, taken from the book *Beside Still Waters*. Copyright © 1984 by Christian Women's Club. Used by permission of the Zondervan Publishing House.

Stamm, Millie, taken from the book *Be Still and Know*. Copyright © 1978 by Millie Stamm. Used by permission of the Zondervan Publishing House.

Stanley, Charles, *How to Handle Adversity,* copyright © 1989, Thomas Nelson Publishers, Nashville, TN.

Steer, Roger, reprinted from *Spiritual Secrets of George Miller,* © 1985 by Roger Steer. U.S.A. rights granted by permission of Harold Shaw Publishers, Wheaton, IL. Worldwide permission granted by Hodder & Stoughton Limited, England.

Steinberger, G., *In the Footprints of the Lamb*, Bethany House Publishers, © 1936.

Stoddard, William S., from the book *First Light,* copyright 1990 by Multnomah Press. Published by Multnomah Press, Portand, OR 97266. Used by permission.

Stott, John, from *Basic Christianity*. Copyright 1958, 1971. InterVarsity Press, London. Published in the U.S.A. by William B. Eerdman's Publishing Co. and in the U.K. by InterVarsity Press. Used by permission. Worldwide permission granted by InterVarsity Press, London, England. Second edition.

Sweeting, George, taken from *The Acts of God*. Copyright © 1986. Moody Bible Institute of Chicago. Moody Press. Used by permission.

Swindoll, Charles R., *The Grace Awakening,* copyright © 1990, Word, Inc., Dallas, Texas.

Swindoll, Charles R., *Improving Your Serve: The Art of Unselfish Living,* copyright © 1981, Word, Inc., Dallas, Texas.

Swindoll, Charles R., *Living Above the Level of Mediocrity: A Commitment to Excellence.* Copyright © 1987, Word, Inc., Dallas, Texas.

Swindoll, Charles R., from the book *Make Up Your Mind,* copyright © 1981. Published by Multnomah Press, Portland, OR 97266. Used by permission.

Swindoll, Charles R., *Strengthening Your Grip: Essentials in an Aimless World,* copyright © 1982, Word, Inc., Dallas, Texas.

Tada, Joni Eareckson, from the book *Secret Strength,* copyright © 1988 by Joni, Inc. Published by Multnomah Press, Portland, OR 97266. Used by permission.

Tamasy, Robert J., (General Editor), *The Complete Christian Businessman,* Wolgemuth & Hyatt, Publishers, Inc. Used by permission.

Tucker, Ruth A., taken from the book *Stories of Faith.* Copyright © 1989 by Ruth A. Tucker. Used by permission of Zondervan Publishing House.

Webber, Robert, *Worship is a Verb,* copyright © 1985, Word, Inc., Dallas, Texas (Second edition soon to be released in 1991 by Abbott Martyn Press, Nashville, TN).

Wenham, David, taken from *The Parables of Jesus.* © 1989 by David Wenham. Used by permission InterVarsity Press, P.O. Box 1400, Downers Grove, IL 60515. Worldwide permission granted by Hodder & Stoughton Limited, England.

White, John, taken from *The Fight.* © 1976 by InterVarsity Christian Fellowship of the U.S.A. Used by permission of InterVarsity Press, P.O. Box 1400, Downers Grove, IL 60515.

Wiersbe, Warren W., Reprinted by permission from *Be Alert.* Published by Victor Books and © 198 by SP Publications, Inc., Wheaton, IL.

Wiersbe, Warren W., Reprinted by permission from *Be Victorious.* Published by Victor Books and © by 1985 SP Publications, Inc., Wheaton, IL.

Wiersbe, Warren W. (Compiler), *Classic Sermons on the Attributes of God.* © 1989 by Kregel Publications: Grand Rapids, Michigan. Used by permission.

Wiersbe, Warren W., taken from *Thoughts for Men on the Move.* Copyright © 1970, 1988. Moody Bible Institute of Chicago. Moody Press. Used by permission.

Wiersbe, Warren W., Reprinted by permission from *Windows on the Parables.* Published by Victor Books and © 1979 by SP Publications, Inc., Wheaton, IL.

Wirt, Sherwood E., *Your Mighty Fortress: Cultivating Your Inner Life With God,* Here's Life Publisher San Bernadino, CA, © 1989.

Wright, Sherwood E., *Your Mighty Fortress: Cultivating Your Inner Life With God,* Here's Life Publishers, San Bernadino, CA, © 1989.

Wright, H. Norman, *Quiet Times for Couples.* Copyright © 1990 by Harvest House Publishers, Eugene, OR 97402.

YFC Editors, from *Practical Christianity;* LaVonne Neff, Ron Beers, Bruce Barton, Linda Taylor, Dave Veerman, and Jim Galvin (Compilers and Editors), © 1987 by Youth for Christ/USA. Used by permission of Tyndale House Publishers. All rights reserved.

Yancey, Philip, taken from the book *Where is God When It Hurts?* Copyright © 1990, 1977 by Philip Yancey. Used by permission of the Zondervan Publishing House.

Yohn, Rick, *Finding Time,* copyright © 1984, Word, Inc., Dallas, Texas.

Zuck, Roy B. (Editor), reprinted by permission from *Devotions for Kindred Spirits.* Published by Victor Books and © 1990 by SP Publications, Inc., Wheaton, IL.

Notes

Notes

Notes

Notes

Notes

Notes